Difficult
How to Surviv

or c ...ucively

Difficult Not Impossible :
How to Survive the Brain Ulcer that is Clinical Depression (and other useful metaphors)

Craig Barton MA (Hons), RMN, MSc

Copyright © 2017 Craig Barton

ISBN: 978-0-244-00563-4

All rights reserved, including the right to reproduce this book, or portions thereof in any form. No part of this text may be reproduced, transmitted, downloaded, decompiled, reverse engineered, or stored, in any form or introduced into any information storage and retrieval system, in any form or by any means, whether electronic or mechanical without the express written permission of the author.

Preface : December 29th, 2016.

I began writing this book in March 2004, following a severe episode of the illness. Inwardly I felt so utterly relieved and thankful to be well again. So, so relieved. Like relief I had never experienced before, like I had been spared the death sentence. Or think of Jimmy Stewart's character at the end of the 1946 classic "It's a Wonderful Life" (but without the singing and revelry). I had been seriously messed and numbed up inside for 3 months - the longest continuous period of clinical depression I have ever endured - and then gradually rediscovered meaning and purpose to my life (or it discovered me). This "renewal" drove me to write lots in a very small amount of time, with the rest following slowly in fits and starts, until this past year's "push to the summit".

In the course of putting this together I have also occasionally persuaded myself to add stuff when actually in the midst of a depressive episode, as - despite problems with impaired concentration, poor motivation, and so on - I think "being in the thick of it" can help to add extra authenticity and accuracy. I hope the final result is better for all the extra years of experience.

Aside from academic assignments and some magazine articles relating to a research post, I have never done any serious writing, and I have never had anything substantial published. I work in the field of psychology but I don't do academic journal writing. Realistically I am not cut out for it as my grasp of research methodology and statistics is pretty average. But I also lack the motivation to try my hand at it, mainly because I know that while a lot of therapists subscribe to journals, not that many actually read them routinely (including myself). As for people who struggle with their mental health, I suspect that only a tiny minority will go near journal articles. So I don't want to sacrifice many hours of my time to have my work effectively gather dust on real and electronic shelves.

But I have always enjoyed writing creatively. In 2004, for the first time, I felt motivated to write something for a wider audience.

My main aim initially was to help my family and close friends understand my illness better, as both I and they often find it difficult to talk about in any depth. In some ways this is helpful, as I wouldn't want to be questioned about it all the time. But overall I am pretty certain we would all benefit from discussing our emotions more openly. It is probably something to do with the complexity of the illness, like where the heck do you start talking about something like this? It is certainly something to do with stigma relating to mental illness. Depression is not something that generally comes easy as a conversation topic. There are too many tricky thoughts and feelings around embarrassment, shame, guilt, vulnerability and weakness.

Another reason for writing this is that I have occasionally been sensitive and defensive at times in my life, often without giving much explanation, so I hope this book can go some way to explain why.

I also think that I have something useful to communicate to other people with clinical depression (whether suffering a single episode or a recurrence). I am proud of what I have written. It is not a perfect account of my experiences, nor my knowledge of self-help and treatments. It is necessarily selective. There will be potentially useful stuff I have missed. But not much, as this is a very thorough book. It also does not flow as smoothly as I would like. But I think it is ok for a first-time author. In my eyes it is good enough. You can decide for yourself.

I decided early on that I would keep the book relatively short and the price moderate. I also decided that I would donate 10% of my book royalties to charity, spread among three worthy UK mental health promoting organisations : *Action on Depression* in Scotland (or equivalent, as I am aware that this charity unfortunately ceased operating in early 2017) ; *Depression Alliance / MIND* in England and Wales ; and *Aware-NI* in Northern Ireland, where I was born. I wanted my book to be readable, accessible and affordable to those in the midst of a depressive episode. This was a clear goal, because I fully appreciate that when you are depressed you can : 1) be put off by a lengthy-looking book ; and 2) be prone to excessive worry about money, with spending on a book feeling like quite a risky thing to do.

Writing a book requires time (although 13 years is probably pushing it ☺). Good health, and peace and quiet, are also very helpful. Of late I have been in the fortunate position to have had all in relative abundance (with the odd blip), which has fostered within me the motivation required to push on, revise, update, and add to the text.

In addition, broadband internet access and the rise of tablet computing have accelerated the whole researching process. All of these factors have combined to help me to finish off and add a little more detail, especially with regard to new approaches to treatment.

In terms of my individual circumstances I am grateful that the NHS in the UK allows flexible career breaks, which allowed me to negotiate a reduction in my full-time working hours for the first 9 months of 2016. Another therapist covered the other half of my hours and gained enough experience to help her gain a place on the Edinburgh University Clinical Psychology Doctorate. My wife Kiran and I had saved up and we cut our cloth appropriately in order to get by over this time. My main goals for this time were simple : write the second half of this book ; catch up with long overdue house maintenance ; spend more time with our daughter ; and organise getting a dog. It has all been done. Thanks in particular to Kiran for being generous-hearted and hard working, and my manager Alison at work for facilitating my temporary part-time hours.

I hope that you find hope and useful advice here.

Acknowledgments

My wife Kiran, daughter Saacha, my mother Jenny, and all of my family, and supportive friends.

Craig Barton,
Livingston,
Scotland.

craigsamuelbarton@gmail.com

NB. Questions, comments, thoughts and constructive criticism all welcome. Also, if you have the time and inclination, a review on Amazon would be much appreciated.

Contents

Introduction 1

Chapter 1 : Be Patient 15

Chapter 2 : Intermittent Battles 29

"Bottom-Up" approaches ⬆

Chapter 3 : Clinical Depression, Medications & Supplements 56

Chapter 4 : Diet 78

"Top-Down" approaches ⬇

Chapter 5 : Thoughts 89

Chapter 6 : Behaviour 103

Chapter 7 : Other Treatments 119

Chapter 8 : Staying Well, New Treatments & Final Thoughts 129

References & Figures 140

Introduction

"Life is suffering. Life is difficult."

Of course not all of the time. Good times are also to be enjoyed. But I think that Buddhist philosophers and Dr. M Scott Peck in his famous 1990's self-help book "The Road Less Travelled" have this about right. Much of life is outwith our control as we are all small parts of bigger systems. Like pinballs in a machine, we are often bounced around at the mercy of other forces. Stressors are hurled at us constantly, often unexpectedly, rendering life difficult and challenging (although ironically if we can accept that life is hard we can often start to cope better). Also at times, through our own actions, and often unwittingly, we trip ourselves up and create our own stress. This applies to all of us, in different ways and at different times.

This book cannot solve everything, as life will of course continue to be difficult. But it can help you to do something about the stuff within your control ; it can assist you to trip yourself up less.

A Bit About Myself

I am prone to a life-threatening chronic health condition which requires sensible management. I have been coping with this since June 1990, some 27 years ago, and I have learned to cope better with time and hard experience. At the same time I still find it extremely challenging and I absolutely dread the sense of the symptoms creeping back in again. But, much like people struggling with hundreds of other life-threatening chronic health problems (diabetes, asthma, crohns, arthritis, to name just a few), sensible management of my condition can result in long spells of good health.

I am not saying that I manage my condition perfectly. Sometimes the life stressors pile up and almost inevitably expose my underlying vulnerabilities. Occasionally I get in my own way and trip myself up with an ill-judged comment. This can lead to excessive worry, which can trigger depression. Often I don't have to say anything ill-judged at all, I will simply obsess about a reasonable comment for no good reason. Equally, passive behaviour can tip me over the edge, like saying yes to a beer when I know deep down I shouldn't, or keeping the peace when I know I would be better expressing my opinion.

However, to the extent that I am responsible for my own health (I guess there are some genetic influences we cannot directly "fix"), I generally cope with stress reasonably well. In the main I take decent care of myself and treat myself with respect, which maximises my chances of good health.

My chronic health condition is **recurrent clinical depression.**

Like many other people with chronic conditions I work for a living. If you are capable of it, it is available, and a robot or computer is not already doing it, work (paid or unpaid) is good for most of us, and that includes me. I manage my condition as best I can, accept my limitations (most of the time) and get on with life. Aside from when I am ill, I don't dwell too much on why I am prone to this difficulty. Life is there for living, in the present moment as much as possible.

I work in the field of mental health. I think there are probably quite a few fellow strugglers / sufferers who also choose to do this, but ironically it is not a subject that is discussed much within our profession. The job I do involves working collaboratively with other people struggling with problematic depression and anxiety, mainly on a one-to-one basis (probably 90% of my work), but also within small group settings (8-12 people). In addition I jointly deliver large-scale stress management lecture courses in the community (prevention being better than cure). Audiences of up to 90 people attend 6 lectures in a block, and these blocks are run 3 times per year in a school theatre in our council area.

The context in which I work is an NHS Psychology Service in Scotland, and my role is a Clinical Associate in Applied Psychology (CAAP). A wordy job title for sure. When the qualifying Masters course was put together in the early 2000's it was proposed that the job title would be Primary Care Psychologist, given that you require a good undergraduate degree in Psychology to do it and the course is of a high quality. But various political discussions blocked that. In essence I do a similar job to a Clinical Psychologist but I work mainly with adults with so-called mild-to-moderate mental health problems, while Clinical Psychologists do more supervision of other staff, and focus on people with severe, complex and enduring problems.

Putting it another way, if you imagine a populations' mental health status represented by a triangle sitting base-up, the mentally well (or at least the ones getting by) occupy the wide base, the people I currently see are somewhere around the middle (where the triangle is significantly thinning), while the severely ill people at the top (or tip) are usually seen by Clinical Psychologists and / or Psychiatrists. I used to work as a CPN (Community Psychiatric Nurse) and Mental Health Nurse, which involved seeing a mix of the moderate-to-severe. So I have worked with people right across the spectrum of mental ill-health.

I imagine that some of my friends and family question my choice of career. I occasionally question it myself. But most of the time my job feels like a good fit, like I have found a decent niche for myself (a small cog in the gears of the various services that provide the "glue" to keep our society functioning reasonably well and peacefully). I remind myself that most of us question our career choices and paths at different times in our lives, no matter what line we are in. I further remind myself that there are asthmatic GPs dispensing advice and prescribing inhalers to fellow asthmatics ; diabetic nurse practitioners specialising in the treatment of diabetes ; physios with dodgy backs doing their best to help patients, and so on and so forth. So, in my eyes it's not such a big issue that a sufferer like myself also works in the field, providing that I regularly remind myself that each person I see is unique and not the same as me. Others will not necessarily require the same approach to getting better as I do, and getting back to voluntary or paid work is not always a realistic and achievable goal.

In addition, it is important for me to acknowledge that I cannot offer a decent service to people if I am ill myself. The blind struggle to lead the blind. I need to be mature and recognise when I am not up to the job. This has resulted in me missing about a week per year on average from my work. I think that I just about make up for that through hard work over the rest of the year, and as I get older my relapse rate is definitely improving (as you will see later, I put this down to better medication, more effective self-help strategies, a more helpful diet, and hopefully a wee bit of wisdom).

Although personal experience does not guarantee effectiveness as a therapist, I think that in my case it is mainly not a hindrance and really does help me to "walk in others' shoes", as far as that is possible. Combined with the belief that I am an important - but relatively small - piece in peoples' jigsaws, I do an effective enough job with the great majority of people I see (I think that some therapists burn out, or are less effective than they could be, because they think they are more important than they really are).

I have enjoyed a varied career so far and have worked with many decent people, both colleagues and patients. I have worked in different parts of the UK in the caring professions for 25 or so years, starting with Bury in Lancashire in 1992, as an Assistant Psychologist in a Head Injury Rehabilitation Unit. I had a tough time with the Lead Psychologist there, mainly because of my own low self-esteem. But I got on with most colleagues and had some very good times. I learned a great deal about the fragility of the brain but also its plasticity, that is its ability to reorganise itself in novel ways following trauma. I went on to work in Oxford as a live-in Support Worker for students with spinal cord-related disabilities. A great experience, also with good times and low times, but mostly within what I would call the blurred boundaries of normal mood variation. In 1994 I undertook a Research Methods MSc at Strathclyde University in Glasgow, but unfortunately struggled more significantly with my mood. About 2 months in to my course I remember taking the decision – a brave one in hindsight – to open up to the 5 random guys I was sharing a university flat with. I decided to be open with them about the fact that I was struggling with depression. I don't think I went on about it excessively, just gave them a brief explanation for my socially avoidant behaviour. They seemed to take it ok (like most people do) and we got on better as a result. The rest of the year wasn't perfect but I know I benefitted from overcoming the stigma of raising the topic of my illness.

It was a tough course though, and not really my cup of tea. I struggled with my thesis. I ultimately decided to defer it in August 1995 and take a working holiday to Australia to see relatives, and explore a bit.

Like many young people I naively thought that I may "find myself" in the process of travel. There were many positives to the trip, amazing family hospitality, some fabulous temporary jobs, but my tendency to depression did not magically lift just because I was ten thousand miles away. You cannot simply run away from your problems ; what goes on on the inside is of utmost importance. Ironically, on my travels, while passing through Byron Bay (a pleasant town near the Gold Coast, kind of new agey and hippified), a chakras therapist first uttered to me the pearl of wisdom that goes ....."the longest journey is between the head and the heart." I didn't really get it at the time. But it stuck, because at some level I knew it was meaningful. Looking back, I was really just at the beginning of that journey, mostly stuck in my head.

Fortunately I did not become severely ill over this time, but I did have some wobbly spells and I think my mood was occasionally of some concern to my relatives. In particular I struggled while working for 6 weeks at a winery in the Hunter Valley in New South Wales. I was living on my own in a nearby small holiday cottage. The accommodation was quite adequate and my cousin's friend – who arranged the job – was a decent boss. Initially all was good, it was a really interesting job, helping with the complex process of turning grapes into wine, but then I fell for one of the girls working there. My low self-confidence got in the way, I could not find the courage to ask her out and I think she may have become more attracted to another guy working there. Or at least she switched off a bit from me. This affected my mood and I then started to struggle to click with my other co-workers. The relative isolation of the place perhaps did not help. I did not help myself at times either, drinking too much on social nights out to try to cope with my insecurities. I also remember getting criticised quite rightly for neglecting to don safety equipment when carrying metal buckets of caustic soda around the winery (used for washing out the tanks). This was low self-esteem at work. I did not value myself enough to adequately manage risk and take care of my own (and others) welfare.

My last month in Australia was spent in Sydney, living with my cousin and working in a call-centre. My cousin was (and still is) really into his fitness and we used to get up most mornings at 6 and go running before work. I have never come close to being as fit as I was then. It helped my mood too. So, overall, a really positive experience, but my gut instinct after 6 months was to return home to the UK. I flew back in the summer of 1996 and just about coped ok for a while, although chucking a waitering job after only 2 days in the job was an early sign that still not all was right with my self-confidence. I could not bring myself to return to my deferred thesis, so I focussed on finding a salaried career. I somehow got a place on the Asda Graduate Management Scheme and started in the September. I lasted about 6 weeks. Crashed and burned under modest amounts of pressure. I felt absolutely sick and tired of myself and the illness. Rationally and intellectually I knew I could cope with the work, but emotionally I was done in. My concentration was so poor, and my confidence so fragile, that I could not even learn how to operate the till properly.

The frustration of what I perceived as yet another "f&*k up" drove me to resign and then spend the following 2 weeks on somewhat of a "mission", researching alcoholism in a quest to understand, accept and forgive my father, who had died a messy alcoholic death 10 years earlier in 1986. A helpful aunt from Australia had sent me a copy of Steve Biddulph's best-selling "Manhood", which recommended doing some homework on your dad if you harboured negativity towards him. This spurred me on to look for answers. I wondered whether, even hoped that, this was the root cause of my problems. I lied through my back teeth to my family, as they thought I was still going to work. An old friend kindly put me up in his flat in Glasgow as I poured over journal articles and books in the Mitchell library ; drove around North Ayrshire visiting pubs my dad used to frequent ; quizzed relatives, friends and acquaintances of his about his demise ; attended AA meetings to get a feel for the addiction ; and other such related activities.

Eventually my researching fizzled out. It had been really useful but was only part of the solution. I retreated back to the family home to lick my wounds where as usual my mum was very patient and supportive. I was as patient with myself as I could manage, gradually got better again, then found a live-in job as a care worker for an old man with Parkinsons. This lasted 7 months, during which time I managed to get a place on the Mental Health Nursing Diploma course at Napier University in Edinburgh.

There started my working in mental health per se. I have been doing so for the past 20 years. Firstly as a Student Mental Health Nurse - both in the wards and community - in and around Edinburgh from

1997 to 1999. Admittedly I got off to a shaky start, having to take 3 months out when depression hit me again. But I got back on the horse again (helped enormously by starting to take prescribed lithium carbonate alongside my antidepressant – see chapter 3), dropped back a class and went on to qualify as an RMN (Registered Mental Health Nurse) in late 1999. My first RMN post was in a Mental Health Day Unit in Barrow-in-Furness, Cumbria. Again, I have many happy memories of colleagues and times spent in a different part of the world. Next I specifically looked for work in the country of my birth, Northern Ireland. It felt like the natural next move. I ended up working in research posts in Derry/Londonderry and Belfast, looking at - among other things - the genetics of alcoholism. This helped me to more fully appreciate the vulnerable, addictive personalities behind alcohol addiction. Interviewing almost 200 alcoholics and their families over the course of a year and a half helped put things more in perspective, to move more in the direction of forgiving my father. My last Community Mental Health Nurse or CPN post was for 3 years in Castlemilk, Glasgow, 2003 - 2006.

In 2005 I successfully applied for the Master of Science (MSc) in Psychological Therapy in Primary Care, run jointly by the Universities of Stirling and Dundee. I undertook this course in 2006-2007. I met the criteria to apply because I have an undergraduate Psychology and Geography Degree from St.Andrews University back in 1992. My Mental Health Nursing qualification and experience as an RMN likely helped too, but was not part of the essential criteria. The course led to that mouthful of a job title of Clinical Associate in Applied Psychology, and I have worked as a CAAP in Primary Care Psychology in the NHS in Scotland ever since.

My current work is mainly guided by Cognitive-Behavioural Therapy (CBT), Behavioural Activation (BA) and Acceptance and Commitment Therapy (ACT), along with aspects of Interpersonal Therapy (IPT), Compassion-Focussed Therapy (CFT), Solution-Focussed Brief Therapy (SFBT), Motivational Interviewing (MI), Assertive Skills Training (a particular favourite - see chapter 6) and Mindfulness. Feel free to do your own research on these approaches. This book includes principles and teachings from all of them, sometimes explicitly stated, sometimes not. On balance I err towards the behavioural side of these therapies. For example, I am guided by teachings such as **"to feel valuable, act like you have** value", "live life to a plan rather than a mood" and "do things in order to feel better rather than wait to feel better before doing things." (I am sure you get the gist. That is, to try as much as possible to rise above your negative emotions - or lack of them – and negative thoughts, and not allow them to always dictate what you do).

In saying all of this, you cannot be an effective therapist by simply spouting theories, quotes and evidence-based coping strategies at people. It is not an exact science and no therapist is perfect. Warmth, collaboration, attentive listening, compassion, empathy, humour, disagreements, annoyance, uncertainty, anxiety, banter, sometimes a struggle to stay awake after lunch..... they are all in there too.

You may have heard of SMART goals : specific, manageable, achievable, realistic and timely. I am also into them. They are a great behavioural tool. That is, to be focussed on the present moment, but with an eye to the short, medium and long-term future. SFBT uses the notion of SMART goals alot. It encourages looking for solutions without reference to the past at all. This can be useful for some. However, I do believe that for most of us it is also important to try to understand our past. We need an appreciation of where we have come from in order to work out where we are going. But in moderation. I do not believe that it is productive to spend too much time dwelling on what has gone wrong, or hunting around in the darkness of our memories, especially in the midst of a depressive episode. When you are well again I think that an *adequate, approximate* understanding of our past is a *good enough* goal to aim for. Better to focus your energies more on where you want to be, rather than where you have been.

A caveat to this is trauma. If there is trauma in your history, if you have experienced or perceived something as physically life-threatening or severely emotionally threatening, it is often useful to look at it in detail. Recall it, talk it through in some detail, however difficult and anxiety-provoking that may be. Go back to the scene of the trauma. Work out if you have been avoiding people, places or situations since the trauma. Start gradually trying to overcome this avoidance. All to work on processing the memory effectively. To help to put it to rest (you will likely need to see a psychologist or CBT-trained therapist to help you to do this).

Now, low self-esteem and depression have affected, interrupted, blighted or tarnished some (certainly not all) of my life and career, but if I focus on the positive, there has been a decent level of occupational success overall. I am also fortunate to feel very grateful for the good times when they come along. **Clinical Depression certainly does not define me**, but at the same time it has played a significant and hugely challenging role in my life.

So, why choose to read my self-help book among the thousands of other useful ones out there? Well, I want this book to be a self-help book with a difference, that strikes emotional, as well as practical and intellectual chords, with sufferers of depression. I want to get across the personal as well as the professional perspective. I want to play my small part in **breaking down the barriers between sufferers and others, between "us and them", as I represent both**. Despite some decent progress in recent years, stigma around mental ill-health remains a significant hurdle to overcome in our society, and we all benefit from chipping away at it slowly.

Besides, struggle and suffering comes with being human. None of us get granted an exemption from it and we can all be challenged in many and varied ways. Some of us get hit by disability or physical ill-health, some of us with psychological problems, some with grief on a scale unimaginable to the rest of us, and some have all of that and more to deal with. We all benefit from airing and discussing our problems at times. In a way, although I would obviously rather enjoy consistently good mental health, I often feel rather grateful in a strange way that my primary health problem is with recurrent depression. Up to this point in my life I have been spared any significant physical illness or condition. This means that I'm essentially "good (enough) to go" every time I emerge out of an episode. I could be so much worse off. Likewise the psychologically resilient person who copes well with a difficult physical disability can have a better quality of life than we may think.

The book might have the feel of part-autobiography, part self-help book, but in essence it is 100% self-help, as reading about my experience can help you. I have lived through the desolation of this illness and I have listened to the stories of thousands of others in the course of my work. I have seen a huge amount of it from both perspectives. **I really do know** that it is **extremely difficult, but not impossible,** to recover from depression (in the following pages you will notice this mantra repeated a lot, intentionally). **You most definitely can survive it and live a meaningful life.**

As I mentioned in the preface, I started to write this a long time ago, in 2004. It has been a stop-start affair. Other things – including loads of wellness - have got in the way and my motivation has waxed and waned. Perhaps predictably, my motivation has tended to rise following an episode of illness, when feeling relieved to be back in the "land of the living". In general, the longer and more severe the episode of illness, the greater the motivation I have had to write. Like the 3 months I literally had "out of it" in early 2004 (see preface) following an experiment with coming off my medication (detailed in chapter 2). 20,000 grateful and relieved words followed in just two months.

More recently I had two significant bouts in 2015 which pushed me further in the direction of finishing this. The first lasted 2½ weeks and was possibly my worst ever in terms of severity, and the second was difficult enough but shorter in duration, and I coped slightly better thanks to a change of antidepressant instigated by the previous episode. If I am honest, although I remain vulnerable to relapse and always will do, this change of anti-depressant has probably led to, on average, a greater stability of mood and improved clarity of thought, helping me to focus on getting this book finished.

Even more recently, in 2017, just prior to publication of this book, I have observed something potentially significant, though at this stage anecdotal and preliminary. 5 months into the introduction of probiotics into my diet, and the signs are really positive. Twice I have relapsed, but instead of a week, I have bounced back within only 2 days (along with challenging my thoughts, pushing myself behaviourally and so on). A decent portion of natural yoghurt and a probiotic yoghurt drink most days, and a miso soup - on average every other day - may be doing their bit to naturally boost my production of mood-enhancing neurotransmitters (see chapter 4 on diet for more detail). In May/June 2017 I actually relapsed more significantly but again coped better than I might have in the past.

Only 3 days were required off work, and although I was fragile for about 3 weeks in total, I still managed to function reasonably well at work and at home.

Main Aims of the Book

The primary aim of this book is to write something down-to-earth and **practical**, because I believe that well-considered **activity** is the no.1 antidote (among others) to depression. I don't mean any old activity, or forcing yourself to run before you can walk. I mean well-thought out activity that is not too threatening, but still gives you a small but significant "therapeutic push" in the right direction. Some of the activity I recommend will simply be activity ; while some will involve recording your **thoughts** in a constructive, helpful manner (of note, I will not be recommending unstructured diary / journal-writing as I believe it can often lead to unhelpful rumination).

Another aim is to flag up the role of **medication**. I believe that it has a significant role to play for the majority of moderate-to-severe sufferers. I believe (along with the UK NICE and Scottish SIGN Clinical Guidelines) that if you are struggling with a moderate-to-severe depressive episode, it is extremely difficult and often impossible to talk your way out of it via self-help and / or psychological therapy.

The "person overboard" metaphor is a useful one here (alluded to on the front cover). Medication can act like a metaphorical lifebelt and help you to keep your head above the water, assist you to swim ashore, and allow recovery to happen (it can also help you to stay well if you choose to take it long-term). Conversely, coping with a serious clinical depression without medication can be like struggling to keep your head above water with heavy boots on. At times you may go under and then surface again, into the "blurred area of normality", feeling just a little bit better (often people say they feel a little better in the evening, only to wake up the next morning feeling bad again). This might happen repeatedly until you feel like you can't take it anymore, you feel like you're drowning. But with agreeable medication you can find the strength to tread water and make your way to safety. Without a suitable anti-depressant you're at risk of drowning. But overall it is worth remembering that anti-depressant or not, **people do usually get better from depression if they can be patient**.

Overall, and most importantly, I want to give **hope** to people who are trying to survive this illness. It is essential for recovery and is in extremely short supply if you are depressed. This illness has come close to prematurely ending my life on a number of occasions but I have always clung on to hope and I have always recovered. I fully intend to survive into my dotage so I encourage you to read what I have to say.

Broadly this book is about helping you, the sufferer of depression, to weather the storm. It's about persuading you to be patient and instil in you just enough hope to choose life for just now. I fully acknowledge how hard it may be for you to keep going. I've been in a similar place too. Most likely not struggling with exactly the same issues or unique variation of depression as you are. But similar enough I would venture, to warrant your continued interest in what I've got to say.

So......... summarising what this book is primarily about :

- **empathising** with your awful situation (and I mean awful, excrutiatingly awful).
- fostering some **hope** in you (as you will be lacking in this crucial attitude of mind).
- suggesting some **practical options** in terms of medication, diet and activity, to help you survive this very difficult time, as your choice of behaviour can positively influence how you think and feel.
- suggesting some ways of **better dealing with your thoughts**, as this can also have significant effects in terms of how you feel - emotionally and physically - and how you behave.

I will go about this by way of the following chapters :

Chapter 1 encourages you to **be patient**, in order to "weather the storm" of depression.

Chapter 2 describes a little of my **personal experience** in order that you can identify with me better. Remember I am both a sufferer and a professional in this field.
Chapter 3 discusses symptoms, **medications**, supplements and other options.
Chapter 4 looks at potential **dietary** changes to help promote positive, incremental change (you may have heard that terminology used regarding the GB Olympic Cycling Team – they left no stone unturned in their quest for success in Rio 2016.... we will try to do the same).
Chapter 5 discusses some helpful strategies for dealing with depressive **thoughts**.
Chapter 6 looks at helpful **behaviours** that "chip away" at the illness.
Chapter 7 will discuss **other treatments** in case the others aren't working.
Chapter 8 will talk about options for **staying well**, potential new treatments and some final reflections for the future.

The chapters are roughly in order of "bottom-up", then "top-down" approaches (see the end of chapter 2 for definitions), but you may have a different outlook. For instance, you may prefer to first read chapters 5 and 6 on dealing with your thoughts and changing your behaviours, as medication and diet may not feel like priorities. Or you may feel like bypassing chapter 2 on my personal experience in order to get on to the stuff that you perceive will help you more directly. You may also judge chapter 7 as not applying to you so much. Whatever you choose, it is 100% valid.

A caveat would be that I would urge you to later return to chapter 2, as it is important that you appreciate our similarities. Similarly, diet and medication are factors way too important to be ignored completely. Whichever way you choose to proceed is absolutely fine, we are all different, and it is impossible to order a book in such a way that suits everyone exactly (not being able to please everyone all the time is a theme we will return to). The emphasis throughout will very much be on **suggestion and empowerment**. I will **not be telling you** to do anything. I will not be using the words **must, should, need to or ought to**. It is ultimately up to you to decide what to try in order to help your recovery. Whatever works in the medium to long term is all that matters (there are short term fixes to depression, for example via illicit drugs, that I would not recommend).

Because your concentration is poor, I'm going to try to keep it relatively brief and concise. Make the paragraphs short where I can. Use short sentences where possible. Repeat certain points from time to time **(eg difficult not impossible).** Try to keep it chatty. For example, not get too worried about grammar, and start some sentences unconventionally with Because, And or But (you may have noticed this already, you may even have been annoyed by it, but at least you now know that it is intentional !). Avoid the over-use of referencing (you can always google stuff later when you feel better). And keep the chapters fairly short so you can pick the book up and set it down more easily.

To finish, it is worth stressing that nowadays I keep in good enough psychological health about 98% of the time. This is not to boast or brag, simply a statement of fact. I believe that this is because I take my prescribed medication (escitalopram, lithium carbonate and omega-3 fish oil supplements) and consistently engage in the behavioural, cognitive (thought-related), and dietary self-help strategies talked about in this book. I only occasionally relapse because : 1) I have a personality that is sensitive to becoming depressed when stressed, and 2) I am human and therefore I make mistakes and miscalculations (I am not self-blaming here, as taking responsibility for one's own health is of paramount importance when managing any chronic health condition). But overall I get by ok.

At the same time I have experienced so much of this illness, tried so many things to help myself, and read so much, that I am in a privileged position to write about the subject. I need to get across the message that it is very **difficult, but not impossible** to survive clinical depression and to constructively manage your vulnerability going forward, via a number of different means. I undoubtedly have some of the solutions, strategies and answers you are looking for. I won't be writing screeds on every potential strategy, as your concentration will be compromised and as you know I am keen that this book is not off-puttingly long. I am aiming to give you information and advice to aid your survival, and leave you to do your own research as appropriate when you feel better again (which will happen).

Chapter 1 : Be Patient

In January 2014 the UK Council for Psychotherapy (UKCP) published a report entitled "Valuing mental health : how a subjective wellbeing approach can show just how much it matters". The authors were Daniel Fujiwara, an esteemed health economist at the London School of Economics (LSE) and Paul Dolan, a Professor of Behavioural Science also at the LSE. They argued that existing methods for valuing the impact of different chronic health conditions hugely underestimated the impact of clinical depression on quality of life. They used an alternative method called the subjective wellbeing approach, which provided persuasive evidence that **our mental health is by far and away the most important aspect of our overall health** (you probably do not need to be told this). They looked at peoples' actual lived experience of 11 chronic conditions and concluded that **having clinical depression is around 5 times worse** than the worst chronic physical health condition. The way they did this was to calculate "monetary equivalent costs associated with different health conditions". That is, not real monetary values, but annual amounts of money that people hypothetically equated their suffering to. A strange way to look at it but the results were striking. Depression came out as "costing" an average of "£44,237" per year to the individual, compared with an annual "£5,556" for the next most challenging physical health category, stomach / liver / kidney / digestive problems.

Now leaving aside complex questions of methodology, this is a huge difference no matter how you look at it. This is not to belittle the challenge of struggling with a chronic physical condition. Living with Multiple Sclerosis, for example, is a challenge requiring a huge amount of courage and continued adjustment, acceptance and commitment. And of course someone may be struck with clinical depression on top of an existing physical condition (this truly must be a nightmare).

Rather, the authors simply wanted to emphasise the plight of the clinically depressed person, because it has been significantly underestimated for years. If you have suffered such depression, or are in the throes of it, or have cared for someone close to you, you will know that this is a meaningful conclusion. **Clinical Depression is an awful affliction that torments and sucks the life out of the**

mind and body. It is a physical, psychological, emotional and psychic illness that is extremely hard to describe to people. A £44,237 "cost" compared with £5,556 probably sums it up as well as anything else.

The famous Pulitzer-Prize winning author, William Styron, himself a sufferer of severe clinical depression, was acutely aware that we are all essentially alone in this life, but that clinically depressed people are way more alone than others. He described depression as "..... a true wimp of a word for such a major illness", a word that "...... has slithered innocuously through the language like a slug, leaving little trace of its intrinsic malevolence and preventing, by its very insipidity, a general awareness of the horrible intensity of the disease when out of control."

With far more literary skill, Styron's writing eloquently reinforces Fujiwara and Dolan's conclusion, highlighting the publics' poor level of understanding regarding what clinical depression actually entails, and how it differs enormously from normal, healthy sadness (given the greater coverage of mental health issues of late, it is probably true that many people are jumping to inaccurate conclusions, labelling themselves as depressed when they are actually simply sad and demotivated). You can extend this to other mental ill-health. OCD is often terribly misrepresented in the mainstream media. For example, the ex-footballer David Beckham apparently has OCD because he lines up his diet coke cans neatly in the fridge. Of course if he is doing this painstakingly and anxiously because he thinks it will protect Victoria and the kids from danger, then this could be described as OCD, but otherwise this is simply about his personality-type preferring neatness and order in his fridge.

Now, I imagine that as you are reading this - whether it be at your local library, in the self-help section of a bookshop, at home, on your tablet, e-reader, or wherever, and you have reached page 16 - you are likely to be somewhere quite far along that depressive "cost continuum", just below or above the "£44,237" level, feeling awful in mind, body and spirit. You are unlikely to be persevering with reading this if you are experiencing healthy sadness. Being like this usually also includes an angst-focussed assessment of whether you want to continue in this world. This is somewhat inevitable when you perceive the illness is "costing you" so much in terms of quality of life. In simple terms, it is excruciatingly painful to be existing. You will probably at the very least have had fleeting thoughts about ending your own life, and at worst you will be actively contemplating it. This may include formulating some sort of a plan, and though you* don't really want to die, and don't want to inflict suffering upon loved ones, it seems like it may be the only way to escape the painful mental torture you are experiencing. You will also likely possess a significantly exaggerated sense of how much of a burden you are on others.

Alternatively you may be reading these words because you have someone close to you who is suffering from depression - or has done in the past – and you want to help them and yourself to cope better.

The harsh reality is that a lot of people with depression do take their own lives**. **Depression can kill.** Worldwide it is estimated that around 1 million people kill themselves every year (WHO, 2015). This is almost equivalent to the population of Greater Glasgow and Edinburgh combined. That is a heck of a lot of people. In 2014 in the UK alone, 6,581 people killed themselves (Samaritans, 2016). While more women than men actually suffer from depression, about 75% (over 4,500) of these deaths were male. Men have a tendency to use more aggressive methods, therefore they 'complete' suicide more often. They also tend to be more socially isolated and less likely to ask for help.

Not everyone who takes their own life will have depressive symptoms to the fore. People kill themselves for complex, multi-faceted reasons, often related to other mental illnesses, debt or terminal illness. And sometimes a person doesn't really mean to do it. Cries for help can accidentally go wrong. For example, the distressed teenager who takes an unintentionally fatal overdose of paracetamol and dies a slow painful death from liver failure. Hopelessness is usually in the mix. So for the majority, at least some of the symptoms of depressive illness are there. One estimate is that 75% of all suicides are linked to depression. Also, at present, 10-15% of people with a recurrent depressive illness go on to kill themselves at some point.

[* footnote : the you I talk of here is the healthy you, the real you that is always at your core, the you who has been struggling to stay afloat, the you who feels like you can't take any more hassle or abuse from the depressive side of you.]

[** footnote : You may notice that I do not use the word "commit" here. I will not be using this word with the term "suicide" in this book because of the connotations with committing a crime. In the vast majority of cases it is a desperate choice of last resort. But, with persistence and patience, it is avoidable.]

Just as startling, around 100,000 suicide attempts or "parasuicides" are made in the UK every year. These attempts are a mix of non-fatal genuine attempts and misdirected maladaptive deliberate self-harm (DSH) (eg someone aiming to cut a vein in order to feel relief from emotional pain but accidentally cutting an artery because of poor knowledge of anatomy).

The above are only the officially recorded figures. The actual numbers are far greater, with some people patching their own wounds up at home or not getting checked out after an overdose. Shame and guilt over their actions are usually involved in the cover-up. Most A&E staff are great, but a few can have rubbish attitudes towards suicide and self-harm, usually borne out of ignorance of mental ill-health and / or frustration over their workload. This puts some people off attending. **Whatever the actual total numbers are, they are not set in stone. There is huge scope for a reduction in numbers.**

There is some good preventative activity going on. Suicide prevention programmes across the country, such as ASIST (Applied Suicide Intervention Skills Training), are attempting to bring down these numbers. In addition, better access to psychological therapies is being provided by IAPT in England and Wales, and developments in Scotland such as CAAP training and more Primary Care Mental Health Teams. The National Curriculum for Excellence in Scotland and parenting programmes UK-wide (such as Triple P and Incredible Years) are all helping to instil more robust self-esteem in our children, hopefully helping them to progress more confidently into adulthood. Free play is being encouraged more in nurseries and the early primary years, as the relationship between this and a healthy internal locus of control in adulthood is better understood. There are health education programmes in schools, and public awareness-raising campaigns such as "See Me" in Scotland. Helplines, charities, voluntary agencies, statutory agencies and our welfare safety net in general combine to provide practical help, advice and support in many and varied forms. Even Facebook has recently developed algorithms that detect subtle suicidal clues in people's online comments – helplines and information are then offered.

With all that in mind you could easily argue the other way : that our suicide figures could be much worse without the various forms of "glue" that keep our society functioning and reasonably cohesive. I would prefer to settle on a political sounding conclusion : we are doing a lot of good things, but I suspect we can do a lot more.

From the macro-perspective it would probably be helpful to have fairer government prioritising less disparity between income levels, while doing all it can to maximise numbers in employment (work generally being good for mental health). Sounds like the ideal combined goal for an unlikely Labour-Conservative coalition ! Joking aside, this is a very complex issue and not one to get bogged down with here. Briefly though, for example, it is generally accepted that raising taxes does not necessarily lead to collection of more tax, as most of us understandably try to minimise the tax we pay. Richer people are better at doing this because they can afford to pay accountants to do it for them. Ideally more people towards the top would realise themselves that they are a lot safer, and society is a lot more stable, when they give up a little of their wealth, and resources are spread more equitably. The more altruistic of us realise that it is beneficial to all of us to spread wealth around a bit. There are also potential benefits to the individual or company in being seen to be generous, charitable and to leave a positive legacy for future generations. There will always be an economic pecking order in life, but philanthropy can help everyone. Historically, Robert Owen of New Lanark and the George Cadbury Bournville chocolate story in Birmingham help to illustrate this. In the present, people like Mark Zuckerburg of Facebook is also showing that you can remain comfortably wealthy while giving lots of money away to worthy causes.

At the same time we probably have to be realistic in accepting that while there is huge room for improvement, unfortunately there will always be people who feel compelled to take their own lives. The harsh truth is that, like other serious illnesses, severe clinical depression can prematurely end lives.

*Unfortunately, once a person is gone there is no way back. The depressed person who takes their own life never gets to discover that they chose a **permanent solution to a temporary problem.** Please think about this. You do not have to become another statistic. You will get better sooner or later, and there is stuff you can do to prevent relapse in the future. Life can be better again. **You can survive this.***

A general downward trend in suicide deaths was observed between 1981 and 2007 in the UK (obs.co.uk). This was helped by the unofficial media code of conduct, with such deaths generally not being publicised (especially the means of death), so as to reduce the copycat phenomenon. But unfortunately numbers have crept up again since then. Perhaps the rise of social media and "compare and despair" interaction, debt and greater socioeconomic inequality are to blame for the rise since 2007. Cause and effect is very complex here and we don't need to get tangled up in it at the moment. But surely we can do better?

Let us see if we can learn anything by comparing death by suicide statistics with another big public health problem, death by road accident. This may sound a bit of a wacky comparison, but bear with me, hopefully it will make some sense.

Suicide statistics for the UK have been rising again recently, but road deaths (including drivers, passengers and pedestrians) have fallen steadily in the UK since the early 1970's. They reduced from over 7,000 in the early 1970's to around 5,000 in the early 1990's. Then the reduction accelerated. By 2013 road deaths were down to 1,713 (gov.uk), despite a huge rise in traffic on the roads (from about 13 million vehicles in 1970 to 35 million in 2013). Injury figures have also mirrored this drop. There are many reasons for this improving picture, including safer cars, mandatory wearing of seat belts, childrens' car seats, better road design, more motorways / dual-carriageways, traffic-calming measures, more cycle paths, better policing and speed camera coverage, and stricter laws on speeding and drink-driving. Perhaps some of our more congested roads are slowing people down more of the time, which is also reducing opportunities for fatal accidents.

It is obvious that a staggering amount of private and public money, thought and planning has gone in to the road safety issue over the past 50 years. Although the public health challenge of road safety is quite a different one, **surely if a similar effort by government, business, local authorities, communities and us as individuals was put into challenging the stigma of mental illness and reducing suicides, numbers would fall from current levels.**

Fundamentally I do believe that the suicide of every clinically depressed person is avoidable, providing the person themselves recognises and takes responsibility for the condition they are struggling with ; and family, friends, communities and society make efforts to overcome the stigma, understand the illness, empathise and ask helpful questions.

I do not believe that anyone suffering from depression takes their own life 100% satisfied that they have made the right decision. There is always ambivalence. There is always uncertainty. The positive, healthy "life-force" is always there, protesting as loud as it can. The "pilot light" is always on. It's just that it can become so muffled and strangled and "oxygen-deprived", that it sometimes caves in to the life-sapping power of the illness.

The waste of human potential is huge. Decent, sensitive, caring, intelligent people are lost forever. The sensitive ones who too often put others first can end up suddenly and shockingly absent from people's lives. And family members and friends (hundreds of thousands of people alone per year in the UK) are left stunned and confused, questioning what they could have done differently. At first glance often it appears that nothing could have been done. However if we look closely it is usually likely that a better understanding of the illness could have helped, along with the courage to ask direct, matter of-fact questions about whether the person is experiencing suicidal thoughts and / or intent.

But, you might say, quite correctly, it is such a difficult illness to understand, it can feel so awkward to ask those sorts of questions. Again I would say **difficult, not impossible.** Of course there are no guarantees, some people kill themselves despite having great support around them. But I would emphasise that asking open, honest and direct questions of a depressed person does not cause them to take their own life. It absolutely reduces the risk of them doing so. It helps them to feel validated. There are too many families and friends who don't ask the right questions. There are too many families and friends who avoid the issue. Unfortunately, if the worst does happen, the questioning and regret suffered by those left behind can continue unabated until they themselves pass away.

We have already focussed on a few statistics. I won't mention many more as your concentration is probably wilting. However one stat I do think is useful is that 5% of people in the UK are depressed at any one time, including all shades of depression, **so you are absolutely not alone** at this moment. Others are battling too. You might benefit from contacting them via a self-help group or internet discussion forum (see chapter 6). You will also likely know that approximately 1 in 4 of the population will suffer from some degree of mental ill-health in their lifetime. That's 25% of people in a similar boat to you at some point in their lives. It really is a bit strange that we don't talk more about our mental health, although to be fair, things are definitely improving in this regard (the first few months of 2017 has seen an increase in campaigns and publicity around mental health).

As well as statistics, another thing we will not be dwelling on excessively in this book is why you are the way you are. In addition to the temperament you were born with, you may have experienced poverty in childhood ; undergone migration ; been separated from your parent/s at an early age ; suffered childhood sexual, physical, verbal or emotional abuse (including neglect) ; been bullied at school ; been pushed too much to achieve at school ; suffered loss and/or bereavement ; inherited some genetic vulnerability ; or some combination of these and many other risk factors. There is strong evidence that adverse experiences such as these will have affected the structure of your developing brain and rendered you vulnerable to mental ill-health in later life. Throw in stress in adult life (eg relating to debt, moving away from home for the first time, an unhappy marriage or partnership, stressful relationships in general, a stressful job or course, unemployment, substance misuse, etc) and you can be more vulnerable to hitting a breaking or tipping point than other people.

What I would love this book to achieve is to help you to recover enough to start exploring these issues, if you choose. **These are extremely important issues** and they are covered extensively in other books and articles. Once you are feeling better it is essential that you gain a better, "good enough" understanding of your root causes, as this will reduce your chances of relapse. Inevitably we will touch on this more in the following chapters. But not excessively so, as investigating the causes of your illness at this moment is not going to help much. To survive this current nightmare you need reassurance and practical advice, with a focus on solutions. You don't need a book as thick as the old-fashioned phone directory, and you cannot do over-analysis of past family relationships at this time. You need to be clearly reminded that people **do recover from depression and can lessen the likelihood of relapse.** You CAN still live a good life. There certainly is a time and a place to explore your roots in order to foster your growth. But this isn't one of them.

You will find that to get yourself well again you will have to take responsibility for your own recovery. When I say this, I mean as much as you possibly can given your present circumstances (depression can be so powerful that even getting out of bed to go to the toilet feels like the most terrifying challenge of your life). In saying this, although you are ultimately in charge, we all benefit from a team on our side. A supportive family is a great asset. Hopefully you have one, but this is not always the case. If you are isolated from support, hold on to the truth that you can still recover on your own, albeit it is tougher to do so **(difficult not impossible).** Your situation may require you to actively reach out and ask for help from other family or friends who have the potential to be supportive. This is of course one of the great difficulties of being depressed, as one of your symptoms (feeling socially avoidant and withdrawing from others) is precisely what you need to overcome in order to help yourself (see more below, under the "The Catch 22's of Depression"). Friends and family you can trust are worth their weight in gold. Your GP and/or psychiatrist, and maybe a Community Mental Health Nurse could be valuable members of your "team". A qualified Psychologist or Counsellor or similar Mental Health Professional can listen, empathise and offer constructive advice. Maybe there is also a local mental health support group or drop-in you can try out (eg Action on Depression in Scotland, Depression Alliance / MIND in England & Wales, or Aware-NI in Northern

Ireland), or a self-help discussion forum on the web (eg on www.patient.co.uk).

However you approach it, "noone is an island", that is we are social beings who generally benefit from social contact (there is a whole psychological therapy named Interpersonal Therapy or IPT based exactly on this premise), even if our depressive side is telling us otherwise. Just being in the company of others **you have chosen to be with** can take your mind off your illness a little. Maybe only a fraction, and you may continue to feel awful and aversive about being in company, but that's better than too much solitary, passive rumination. The latter can lead to the depression taking a tighter grip.

The Catch 22's of Depression

Part of the way through my tussle with the illness in 2004 I came across an article whilst trawling the internet, by a Dr. Jon Allen, a Senior Staff Psychologist at somewhere called The Menninger Clinic in America. From academic, work and personal standpoints I have read hundreds of books and articles over the years concerning the predicament of the depressed person, but none have struck a chord with me so much as this one. To me, he writes brilliantly. Of course, it is such an individual illness that what he says may not feel as relevant to your situation, or some of it will and some of it won't, but here's a few excerpts anyway. Assess for yourself.

You will also plainly see that the title of this book was inspired by his writing.

"The plight of the depressed person is not fully appreciated........"

<u>"Severely depressed persons are between a rock and a hard place. Let's first consider the rock :</u> Depression is an acute illness, like the flu, from which you recover quickly. Many persons who have struggled for a long time to overcome depression have been urged by others, "If you'd just (eat right, go out and exercise, have more fun, stop isolating, etc)... you'd feel better". I've come to think of "just" as a fighting word - it's

inflammatory to persons who have lived with depression and have tried to fight their way out of it with limited success. There's no single, simple solution to persistent depression. You must work on it on several fronts. It can be a long haul, even if you're able to put a lot of effort into it.
Here's the hard place : Depression is a serious, persistent, mental-physical illness. I think the hard place is a more realistic place to be than the rock. Depression is a serious illness, recovery may take a lot of time, and you remain vulnerable to recurrence. This is a hard place indeed, but sitting on the rock is potentially crazy-making - you should be able to snap out of it, but you cannot. Therefore you conclude that you are crazy, lazy, or some other depressing idea".

"Depression is a hard problem. Why does it take so long to recover? Why is it so difficult and painful? Here's the rub : All the things you need to do to recover from depression are made difficult by the symptoms of depression! For example, if you're depressed, it's likely that you've been severely stressed and feel exhausted. Therefore you must rest. But consider one of the most common symptoms of depression : insomnia. A Catch 22. There are many others. You should eat well, but depression decreases your appetite. You should be active - even exercise! - but depression robs you of energy. You should participate in enjoyable activities, but depression erodes your capacity for pleasure. You should think realistically, but depression brings negative thinking. You should spend time with family and friends, but depression prompts you to withdraw and isolate. Above all, you should stay hopeful, but depression may bring hopelessness.

Contemplating the Catch 22's of depression is risky - potentially adding to your discouragement. Keep in mind that it is not impossible to recover from depression, despite the Catch 22's. We know this because people do recover. Recovery is difficult, but not impossible. Making the distinction between difficult and impossible is crucial to recovery. Recognising the difficulty may be discouraging, but failing to recognise it can be even more demoralizing. Minimizing the seriousness of depression leads to unrealistic expectations, enormous frustration, self-criticism, and hopelessness - all of which add further fuel to depression.

You may criticize yourself - or be criticized by others - for wallowing in depression. But you did not choose to be depressed, and you cannot simply choose to be depressed no longer. You cannot just make up your mind to be well and heal yourself by some act of will. But, if you're not profoundly depressed, you can choose to take actions that will take you slowly along the path of recovery. <u>Recovering from depression involves a series of hard choices over a long period.</u> It can be a hard choice to get out of bed, take a shower, to get dressed, to go for a walk, or to call a friend. You cannot choose to recover from depression at one moment, once and for all. Recovering from depression requires making hard choices continually, one after the other, day after day, month after month. <u>It's like climbing a mountain, with ups and downs, gains and setbacks along the way.</u> The more depressed you are, the harder the choices, the harder the climb. As you respond to treatment, the choices become easier, and you have more strength and ability to climb.

Keep in mind the Catch 22's. It's hard to climb a mountain when you're exhausted. One of the most demoralizing aspects of depression is its persistence and recurrence. <u>The main implication of having a persistent illness is this : You must take care of yourself in the long run.</u> Yet another Catch 22 here is that you may feel like you're not worth caring for if you're depressed. Many persons have worked hard and successfully over a long period of time to fight depression. They become demoralized when they become depressed again after all the hard work they've done in the past. They've climbed so far only to fall off a cliff. "I'm tired of fighting it. I can't go on fighting". No wonder some depressed persons feel like giving up entirely. Depression is frustrating."

"Within each of the Catch 22 areas, you have some leverage over depression. The leverage is not great - you can't just "snap out of it", no matter how much you wish to do so. Fortunately, however, we are not dealing with black and white, but rather shades of grey. You need to be motivated to recover. You need energy to be motivated. If you're depressed you may have little energy. But you're likely to have some energy and some motivation. It's these shades of grey - however dark - that make the Catch 22 problems very difficult rather than utterly impossible. You have a little leverage in many areas......

You will notice that I have underlined some key points :

"Keep in mind that it's not impossible to recover from depression despite the catch 22's. We know this because people do recover. Recovery is difficult .... not impossible."
These words resonated with me when I read them, so much so that they inspired the title of this book, and I am repeating them regularly throughout. I knew them to be true already, but to hear them from someone so insightful was very powerful.
Of note, the notion of the multiple double bind or "catch 22" was inspired by Joseph Heller's famous novel from 1961.

All the things you need to do to recover from depression are made difficult by the symptoms of depression. So true.

Recovering from depression involves a series of hard choices over a long period. You need to keep chipping away.

It's like climbing a mountain, with ups and downs, gains and setbacks along the way. Recovery is rarely a smooth emergence out of the dark and into the light. Like recovery from any illness – physical or mental – we have good days and bad days, but ultimately take more steps forward than back.

The main implication of having a persistent illness is this : you must take care of yourself in the long run. Much of this book has to do with taking care of yourself in order to promote recovery. However, most of what is covered can also be applied to staying well in the future. If I am honest with myself I know that I have not looked after myself as well as I could have since being diagnosed in 1990. I have done a reasonable job of coping with a chronic condition, but I acknowledge that I can always do better.

Actually, I said excerpts, but the above is pretty much most of his article. There are small bits that don't pertain to me. For example, there was a paragraph on appetite being stifled by depression, but mine probably increases if anything, in a comfort-eating sort-of-a-way (I think this relates to the common physical symptom of the senses being dulled, in this case my sense of taste, leading to eating more food, quicker). There may be parts which don't strongly relate to you either. For example, some people sleep a lot when depressed rather than struggle with insomnia. But I generally think Dr. Allen writes so well that it's hard to leave bits out. He covers all the main symptoms of the illness and eloquently describes the frustration felt by sufferers.

Dr. Allen pretty much sums up my approach to tackling this illness : that is, by working on the areas you have a little leverage over, by "chipping away" (see the front cover), you will gradually climb back up the mountain to recovery. You will likely experience setbacks on the way, but eventually you will get there. Dr. Allen has written loads more since 2004 and I would recommend that you read some of his stuff at your own pace.

Hopefully by the end of this book you will feel a little more hopeful. I cannot guarantee that you'll be feeling much better (we both know depression is often very persistent and powerful, and that sometimes we can feel a little better at night, only to wake up back at square one). But maybe you'll be thinking... *"I can recover from this hell"* ; that it's going to continue to be **very difficult, but that *it's not impossible*** to get better. Depression is not a terminal illness, though you could be forgiven for thinking so in the midst of an episode. You may have recovered before ; you will do so again. If this is your first bout, you *can* recover, many others have before you. You will have good times again.

As you read on, have in mind the old 19th century Irish proverb **"the darkest hour of all, is the hour before the day"**. In terms of the struggle with depression I believe it often to be true.

I will start by letting you know a little of my own struggle with the illness. As said, if you are desperate to get started on coping strategies you may prefer to jump to another chapter, which would be fine. However I think it is important for me to include a personal chapter, by way of letting you know where I am coming from and that I have some idea of what you are enduring.

Chapter 2 : Intermittent Battles

Early Days

I was a happy enough child, pretty easy-going by most accounts. I generally did well. I won the handwriting prize twice in a row in my early years of primary school. I was towards the top of the class most years. I won the "Best Boy" prize at the Sparks Boys Club when I was 8 (I remain amazed at how I managed to do a forward roll after diving over 8 other boys in the gymnastics display). We moved house from Glasgow, to Troon in Ayrshire when I was 9, and I coped fine with that. I continued to do pretty well at school and made a decent amount of good friends. I played lots of golf and tennis in the summers and went on some great camps with the scouts. My transition over to secondary school went pretty smoothly. I was not subject to any chronic bullying. I was involved in 2 or 3 fights at school in my early teens, and usually lost – I wasn't a soft touch but I wasn't really a fighter either. I worked hard and got good results in my important school exams. I was vice-captain of the rugby

Me (middle) with James Ritchie (right, also a golf bursar), the St. Andrews University Principal in the gown, the Head of PE and the then captain of the R&A Golf Club (Michael Bonallack) on the left. Check out my troos ☺ (1988)

Me on the 18th fairway, Old Course, St Andrews(1988)

team and head-prefect in my sixth year. I wasn't the most popular guy in town, but I think I was liked well enough by most of my peers, and disliked by few. That's probably what gets most head prefects elected. I achieved a good enough set of Scottish Highers to gain entry to study Psychology and Geography at St. Andrews University. I also developed my golf game well enough to be awarded a golf bursary for my four years at St. Andrews. £1000 per year (a decent chunk of money in those days) to spend on competition entry fees, travel costs, coaching and equipment. An amazing opportunity.

I gave up the golf bursary after year one. Many people were, not surprisingly, surprised at my decision. My competition scores had been poor on average but there had been a few decent performances to perhaps build on. I was never going to be a professional, but this was a great opportunity to maximise my potential and play at a decent amateur level. Essentially, low self-esteem had kicked in. Or perhaps it would be more accurate to say it had been there for a while, but had now been exposed. I put too much pressure on myself to perform well. I worried excessively about how others saw me. I struggled to adapt to the changes suggested to me by my coach. These suggestions may in fact have been the wrong ones for me, but I did not have the self-belief to say so. I focussed excessively on my perceived failures and shortcomings and minimised any positives. I did not feel worthy of the award.

One particular story illustrates my low self-esteem really well I think. I played in the Scottish Boys Golf Championship at Dunbar as a 16 and 17 year-old. It was straight knock-out. I lost both times in the first round. The first time was a close match, never too much in it either way, but the second time was an awful experience. My dad had died 4 months previously. I was playing for him as much as myself. I played really well for 12 holes and was 5up with 6 to play against a guy from Duddingston in Edinburgh (if you don't know golf, suffice to say I was well ahead and surely could not lose). I proceeded to absol-utely, pos-i-tively, bottle it big time. I got very nervous. Before I knew it, I had lost 5 holes on the trot and stood on the 18th tee all square (even). I was sh**ting it. He didn't even play the last hole very well. All I had to do to at least extend the match to extra holes was to extricate myself from a greenside bunker and 2 putt. Like something out of a perfectly scripted golfing disaster movie, I thinned that bunker shot over the 18th green, over the course boundary wall, out of bounds. I shook hands in defeat. I remember, shellshocked, going for a coke in the clubhouse afterwards and overhearing the bar staff discussing my capitulation, news of which had travelled quickly. Humiliation does not come close to describing how I felt. I still feel painful emotions recalling this.

Only a game of golf of course......... but emotionally very much intertwined with my upbringing. I felt like I had embarrassed myself and let my dad down badly.

A story to keep to oneself you might say. A story to only repeat occasionally to trusted friends and family as a reminder of sport's ability to humble. Well, not for me. In a misguided attempt at getting people to like me, I told this story numerously over the next few years. Others laughed with me, and at me, as I did so. I metaphorically brought my self-esteem down a notch every time I rolled that story out. Or to be more precise, every time I told the story without providing the important context to it. Namely that my father had died 4 months beforehand and I was grieving and fragile at the time. A few years later in a university team match in my 3rd year, I even recounted that story to my opponent on the 8th fairway of the St. Andrews New Course. What a way to intimidate your opponent ! Turned out to be the very same guy from Duddingston who had beaten me 4 years earlier ! I had not recognised him. Suffice to say I didn't win that day either.

The close cousin to the frequent repeating of a disaster story is the "not saying anything" option. I further unwittingly drove my self-esteem south by also playing down any successes I had at that time. For example I rarely mentioned to anyone that I dusted myself down from that defeat and went on to win the Individual Trophy at the Golf Foundation Scottish Schools Team Championship at St. Andrews the following week. Or if I did mention it I would highlight the lucky breaks I had in doing so, minimising what was a decent achievement. I opted out of many conversations with friends and family, too often going with feelings of inadequacy and thoughts of "my story or point is not good enough / funny enough / interesting enough to bother them with".

This is what my father taught me whether he meant to or not. Fortunately this stuff can either be unlearned or worked around (to be honest, I think it is very difficult to shake off early teachings completely, but they definitely can be worked around).

This **low self-esteem morphed into intermittent clinical depression** from aged 20, midway through my university years, at the end of my 2nd year. University friends were perplexed at how I could be just about ok one week, and low, avoidant and distracted the next (actually, I don't know if they were puzzled for sure, as my problems were not talked about very much, but I assume at least some friends felt this way). They didn't know my back story, they didn't know my baggage. I fell off a lot of peoples' radars. I sometimes drank to excess in a vain attempt to cope better, but I often ended up making a fool of myself and it always made things worse. Many friends gradually distanced themselves (along with me distancing myself from them), unsure of how to help, and with their own struggles and challenges to deal with. Somehow I went on to earn an honours degree, but at a level way below what I was capable of.

I have battled on since my first episode of depression. I have been reasonably successful in life. I have worked hard to achieve what I have. **However any hard work involved, pales in to absolute insignificance compared to the work required to survive a bout of clinical depression.** The following attempts to describe the undescribable symptoms.

Just uncurling myself from the tensed up foetal position to step out of bed in the morning becomes an enormous, frightening task. Like I'm going to be stepping into piranha-infested waters or hot lava. And that can be after waking at 3 or 4 in the morning, highly anxious, agitated, full of dread, knowing that the nightmare of continued living is still with me. Sometimes the illness plays with my mind at night, allowing me brief episodes of dream sleep where I imagine I am back to normal, feeling in control, on top of things...... and then I wake up to the tormented reality. When I can postpone it no longer, I force myself out of bed to have a shower, maybe a shave, get dressed, have some tasteless breakfast, and so on with the aching numbness. All the routine tasks usually done instinctively and contentedly on auto-pilot become insanely difficult to accomplish due to a lack of motivation, impaired concentration, indecision and a stifling sense of meaninglessness. The lack of energy ; the wracking feelings of shame and guilt ; the lack of interest in usual things (I can't be bothered with golf, it does not appeal anyway, everything feels pointless, especially hitting a wee white ball into a stupid round hole, I feel too scared, worried of what people will think of me if I'm seen on the course, I would play badly anyway because of my awful concentration......) ; the numbness ; the blandness ; the sluggishness ; the clumsiness ; the self-hatred ; the over-sensitivity to some people's comments ; the awful worrying regarding some of my own comments (usually made just before becoming ill), occasionally spilling over into paranoia ; the preoccupation with my flaws and faults ; the obsessive worry over ridiculous notions ; the dominance of unhappy memories in my mind ; the aversion to others because of the deep shame over the way I am ("they must be able to tell I am fu**ed up").... the generally weird perspective I have, the lack of connection I find so difficult to describe to others................the terrifying temptation to take my own life...... it all adds up to something very difficult and painful, very difficult to describe in words, an existential-sort-of-crisis, yet way more than that.

Or maybe "£44,287" sums it up better.

A Bit of Analysis

I am unsure how exactly I became susceptible to the illness. I obviously cannot say it was 50% because of this and 25% because of that. However I am sure that it was down to a combination of various factors, possibly some genetic inheritance, and definitely including experiences in my formative teenage years.

I was the first-born son with two younger sisters. My father was a big, handsome man with a corny sense-of-humour. He was also a keen golfer, I think his lowest handicap was 3 or 4. He was an active dad with fairly high standards of behaviour. He studied chemistry at university but dropped out and got into sales repping with Texaco. He realised in his mid-30's that he could make more money from running petrol stations, so he took the risk and changed direction. It paid off and initially he did well. I was aged between 5 and 9 around

My father, Brian Barton, in good health, receiving a prize at a Texaco Golf Pro-Am tournament (c.1973).

this time. My younger sister and I were expected to do chores around the house and garden. Nothing of Dickensian proportions, but enough to "keep our noses clean", as the old saying goes. We also helped out at his work, cleaning the petrol pumps, re-stocking the shelves and such like. He wanted (and expected) a lot of me academically, and in the sporting arena. There was definitely an element of wanting me to succeed more than he had – not unusual of course. Besides I was generally well-behaved and keen to show him I could do well.

Actually I absolutely idolised him, depended on him, and in many ways saw him as a good friend. He ran me to golf competitions, supported me, praised me and rewarded me when I passed exams and did well at things. We played a lot of golf, pool and snooker together.

He always drank a fair bit. Sometime in the mid-to-late 1970's he developed a fondness for Carlsberg Special Brew, a superstrength lager. He had been overweight for as long as I could remember, although there were photos of him as a slim, handsome, athletic-looking man when he married my mother in 1969. Overweight became obese and bloated around 1983-84 (when I was 13 or 14), then a slow loss of weight began. In June 1986, 6 months before his death, he was jaundice, unsteady, ruddy in complexion and thin. He occasionally posed deludedly in front of the mirror proclaiming that he was getting back to his "fighting weight". He became quite sensitive - bordering on paranoid - about "the people in the West of Scotland" being overly-critical, and would go on about such people talking too much about themselves. He would impress on me to "always ask questions" of others. This was not necessarily unhelpful advice and has certainly proven to be useful in my chosen career, but my take-home message was very much focussed on "I should be overly modest, self-deprecating and not talk about myself too much". He developed unhelpful views on many topics, which I inevitably took on board to some degree and still have to work around to this day.

Latterly he hit my mother on a few occasions, which was way out of character for him. My mum told me later he started to wet the bed at times. His blood's ability to clot was affected. When he cut himself shaving he wouldn't stop bleeding, his face dotted with bits of toilet paper to stop the blood. He died through horrible, alcohol-related complications when I was 16, oesophageal viruses rupturing, throwing up sinkfuls of blood clots before being taken away to hospital. My sister and mum had to deal with the horror of all that. I was out volunteering on the Round Table Christmas Lorry dressed as an elf collecting donations and missed the gory stuff. He died a day or two later on 21st December 1986. It's all a bit of a blur. He was only 44. My mum was only 40 and my sisters were 15 and 6. Our family GP told me years later that she had never dealt with such a severe case of alcoholism as my father. I interviewed just shy of 200 alcoholics in Ireland as part of a research post in 2001-2002, and while there were many who could match him for dependency, his body simply could not take the punishment.

He was generally a good man and decent father. On the other hand, latterly he was chaotic, selfish, deceitful and properly f**ked up. On more than one occasion after helping him at work, I had to steer the car 12 miles home for him while he operated the pedals, because he was too drunk. He took me into gloomy, run-down pubs where he usually sat alone doing the crossword, by that time chasing his Special Brew with whisky. A previously gregarious and sociable man reduced to a physical, psychological and emotional shadow of his former self. We all went to the international rugby at Murrayfield once and he fell asleep during the match. Not so much a snooze, more of a light coma, requiring help from other adults in our party to get him back to bed in the hotel before we had even had our dinner. He bet on the horses too much, he took increasing risks on dodgy stockmarket investments, his business suffered. His decline almost perfectly matched the first half of the U-shaped curve described in Max Glatt's reknowned early work on alcoholism. Except that my dad hit rock-bottom and kept on going. There was no "sudden shift" or realisation of his perilous situation, followed by gradual recovery. There was no metaphorical parachute that opened up to cushion his descent. He hit the ground like the coyote in roadrunner. Splat. After his death mum filled 2 binbags with empty cans of Special Brew found hidden around the house and garage. His demise was so relatively rapid that, unlike many bereaved families of addicts, there was actually a bit of money left over to cushion the financial blow. If his constitution had been stronger he likely would have drunk and gambled the lot, because addiction does that.

His death was a genuine shock to me. Because of my age and personality I was blind, in denial, or both, to the severity of his decline over his last few years. I knew he wasn't well, but I had formed only a basic concept of alcoholism as an illness or disease. I couldn't really get my head or my heart around his situation. Plus I'm not sure the family talked about it much. Understandably my mother wanted to protect us, and my sisters and I avoided facing up to the elephant in the room. With the help of an old friend of my dad's, efforts were made to get him to attend Alcoholics Anonymous, but I think he only attended once. In his eyes there was absolutely nothing wrong with him, everyone and everything else was to blame. Such was his level of denial and delusion.

Of course I can only guess at the reasons behind his demise (and my own problems for that matter). As illustrated by the Johari Window (see figure 1), there is much I do not know about him (and myself)f. There is stuff that he knew and others did not. Stuff that others knew and he did not. Stuff that no one knew. Complex genetic factors. The influence of his early life. His sensitive personality. The relationship with his parents and brother. The culture of the times, and so on.

Figure 1 : The Johari Window

Johari Window

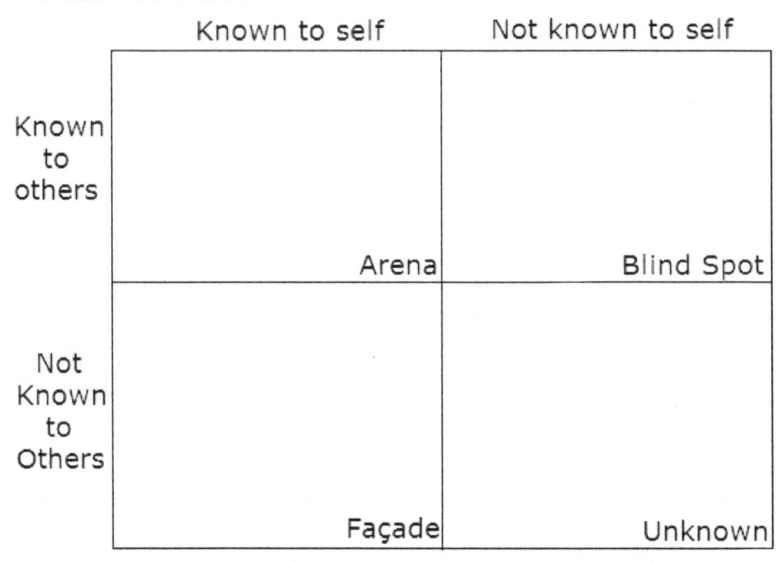

	Known to self	Not known to self
Known to others	Arena	Blind Spot
Not Known to Others	Façade	Unknown

In hindsight his death was predictable, given the abuse his body had endured, but at the time it was a bolt out of the blue. His behaviour had left me very confused inside. As Dorothy Rowe says in her book "Depression : The Way Out Of Your Prison", I had built a picture of how I thought my world was, but in reality it was very different. Where previously I had thought dad was simply keen to spend time with me, I started to face up to the unpalatable truth that there will have been times when my dad's primary motivation for a game of pool or snooker or whatever, was to get out of the house, away from his responsibilities, to drink.

In terms of personality development, if you believe that most people form the foundations of their personalities from the vicarious observation of their main role-models, then unfortunately it was almost inevitable that my foundations became inherently unstable, vulnerable and prone to buckling under stress. I observed and learned from my father, this helped to form the foundations of my personality, and despite adding my own unique personality on top, my foundations remained wobbly (see Steve Biddulph's excellent best-seller "Manhood" for a male perspective on this).

Following his death I got on with things as best I could. I remember crying myself to sleep the night he died, but then I put a lid on it. I felt I had to be the (young) man of the house. I felt I had to be strong for my mum and sisters. I felt I had to help with the closure of dad's business (in reality I could not do much in this regard, but fortunately we had help from the same good friend of my dad who had tried to persuade him along to AA). I pushed myself to get my head down to study for my Scottish Prelim Exams in the January of 1987, followed by my important Higher Exams in the spring of that year. I wanted to succeed in honour of my father. And I did. At the time I still saw him through rose-tinted glasses.

Let's go out on a bit of a tangent for a moment (try and humour me here). Some of you may remember the film "Predator" with Arnold Schwarzenegger, which also happened to come out in 1987. A team of grizzly veteran soldiers are dropped into a steaming jungle in the middle of nowhere to find out what has been killing the locals. Arnie's in charge of course. It turns out that Jean Claude Van-Damme's character, a scary looking invisible alien, is causing all the mayhem and bloodshed. As might be predicted, bad-ass alien starts bumping off grizzly soldiers one-by-one in pretty quick succession. One of the soldiers, Mac, played by Bill Duke, utters the classic under-stated line "I aint got time to bleed" after cutting himself shaving, in the knowledge that the Predator was close-by. Despite such a classic line, unfortunately he too soon bit the dust.

Reigning that tangent back in again, it literally was like in early 1987 I was saying to myself "I aint got time to grieve". I felt I had to get the head down, press on and succeed. But it all came at a cost.

I coped pretty well as an outgoing chirpy-chappy, people-pleasing, slightly insecure and under-confident type of character, until I was 20. You might recall that at 19 I gave up the golf bursary, and with that perceived stressor removed, 2nd year at university subsequently progressed ok. I had minimal confidence with women and generally avoided closeness, but I bumbled along fine for most of that year.

Then I found myself falling in love with a girl in my Hall of Residence. Being of low self-esteem this love had an obsessive quality to it, with the object of my affection positioned well above me on a metaphorical pedestal. It turned out to be unrequited love, and I just couldn't cope. She was still fine to be friends, but my low opinion of myself meant I felt irrationally rejected. I knew in my head I was overreacting, but my heart was broken and I felt worthless. My underlying low self-esteem rendered me vulnerable to something most young guys would have just shrugged off.

I headed out to America during that summer of 1990 to teach golf at a summer camp for Jewish children. In hindsight maybe I would have been wiser to stay at home, but it was all organised and paid for, and as was probably said at the time, I would surely cheer up when I got there. But my self-confidence was at an all-time low. I became very homesick and struggled to deal with the duties of my job. I couldn't understand why I was feeling empty and tearful so often. I could not make anything more than superficial friendships with my peers. I felt extremely lonely. The general enthusiasm for life and uber self-confidence displayed by most of the children in the camp only served to make me feel even more inadequate. I drank too much on some nights out with staff, hoping in vain that I might feel better. I slipped into clinically depressive territory for the first time about halfway in to my 8 week stay, seriously questioning the meaning of my life, other peoples' and the world around me. I swung between this and a very fragile, borderline confidence for the rest of the summer, and into my final two years at university.

I could analyse the causes of my depression into infinity. It is of course possible that I could have suffered from the illness even if my father had been a tee-totaller and alive and well today. But I very much doubt I would have developed such a serious recurrent illness without the stress exerted on my system by my father's behaviour . His demise was a devastating blow. After all I was a fairly confident and able child. For 13 or 14 years I had been well nurtured and brought up on the whole. I consider myself very fortunate in this respect, as many people endure abuse and neglect from the word go in life. But it is likely that the experience of witnessing my father's tortuous physical and psychological decline, combined with my own sensitive "peace-keeper" personality, tendency to keep my emotions to myself, and a lack of open discussion within the family, was enough to lead to changes in my developing brain's chemistry. Thus rendering me more vulnerable than most to depression in adult life.

In other words, it wasn't his actual death that part-caused my depression, it was my inaccurate appraisal of his self-destructive behaviour in the lead up to it, and my continued misinterpretation of these events afterwards. As the idealised memories faded, I began to feel betrayed. On balance I still have to conclude that in some ways I was let down by him, while in other ways I acknowledge that he was simply consumed by a rampant addiction. Other friends lost their fathers prematurely around the same time but they did not go on to develop depression like me. Whilst my personality-type likely rendered me more vulnerable than them, another key difference was that these guys' fathers died of illnesses like cancer and heart disease. Illnesses perceived as not their own fault, or outwith their control. And not involving chaos, lying, deceit and self-harm.

Perhaps if my father had lurched on like most alcoholics I would have "woken up" to his behaviour and challenged him, got some of my anger out. I think he probably died at the worst possible time for me. My shell-shocked mum was so affected by it all that she rebounded into the arms of a dodgy car salesman, a guy with his own problems who had served with the British Army in Northern Ireland. He was champing at the bit to move in with her, and I think my mum was understandably looking for affection after years of unhappy marriage. To my mum's credit she chose to give us all a fresh start, moving us to a new house elsewhere in our area. He moved in with us too soon, about 15 months after my dad's death. My fledgling status as (young) man of the house thereby ended pretty quickly. I pretty much went along with it all, pleasing my mum, while really not wanting him to be there, feeling uncomfortable with the presence of this guy. He was an opportunist who left his first wife and young kids at least partly for the financial stability inherent in my mother's situation. I should have said more, but I did not have the self-confidence.

Perhaps uncles and old friends of my father could have guided me a little better, but in those days it was less of the done thing. They may have tried a little, but I may not have been very open to receiving help at that time. After all, on the surface I was doing alright (to start with). They also had their lives to deal with, mortgages to pay, children to raise and so on.

I do remember writing to one old friend of my father when I was depressed at about age 21, who replied to me with a very thoughtful letter, but could not bring himself to say that my dad was an alcoholic. Out of misplaced good intentions he described dad as probably going through a spell of mid-life boredom with his work, as if that was enough to explain drinking himself so aggressively to an early grave.

Ideally I would have seen a bereavement counsellor and / or therapist. We all should have. Or even attended a support group like Al-Ateen or Al-Anon. My younger sister coped differently, not ideally, but probably more adaptively, generally shunning my mum's new partner. My youngest sister being only 7, wasn't sure which way was up. Both of my sisters at least benefited from their main female role-model battling on with life. My mother is a complex and sometimes frustrating personality, but very loving and supportive and made of stern stuff ; someone who frequently battles with anxiety, but keeps pushing on. To her huge credit she continues to work part-time as a sales assistant with Marks & Spencer at the age of 71.

Here is a crucially important point. All of the above type of analysis is fair enough when you are well. However, when you are in the throes of a clinical bout of depression it does not pay to dwell. In fact, I have found it somewhat counter-productive to analyse too much when I am unwell. Sports Psychologists sometimes use the term "analysis-paralysis" to describe sportsmen and women overly bogged down by the fine detail of how they are performing. I think you can also apply this meaningfully to being in the midst of a depressed spell. Best leaving the analysis to when you feel well. Even then, you may or may not find there are major revelations to be uncovered.

Break it Down and Problem-Solve

No matter how supportive your "team" of family, friends and others, if the illness persists for any length of time there is a temptation to duck out of life, to end the torment. In the past I have nearly chosen this option. Fortunately I am still here. Likewise, I hope you can resist that temptation if it is present.

Human-kind has evolved to where it is today by solving problem after problem, often in new and innovative ways. As alluded to in the introduction, In his famous and occasionally insightful book "The Road Less Travelled", M Scott Peck makes reference to the ancient Buddhist principle that 'life is suffering'. At face value this sounds a bit harsh, but what he basically means is that life is very difficult. It is essentially a series of problems to be solved, some big, some small, most inbetween, one after the other. And most of us get our fair share thrown at us. Life can be enjoyable of course, but noone can avoid problems, noone gets off scot-free. Acceptance of this fact is enormously helpful for everyone. Life was never meant to be easy.

Essentially this depression you are struggling with, is a BIG, COMPLEX problem (albeit it feels pretty huge and insurmountable at the moment), so there are solutions to be thought of, considered and tested out. 'Survival solutions' if you like. Some of these will help more than others, some may not seem to help at all. Discard the ones that definitely don't help, and continue with the ones that do help, or at least might do.

Putting them into practice is **difficult, but not impossible**. 'Survival solutions' vary between individuals. After all, you are a product of a unique genetic make-up and upbringing. As the famous conductor and cellist Pablo Casals was once quoted as saying, there is no one person exactly the same as you in the world. But we all have enough in common that at least some of the solutions I will talk about later will be relevant to your recovery. It's a bit like the plumber or joiner choosing tools for a job. The question is, which solutions will you pick for the job of surviving this nightmare? We will discuss your options from chapter 3 onwards.

Two Near Misses

I am not going to put my experience of depression into chronological order and detail every episode. That would not be appropriate here, as this is not an autobiography, and as mentioned I don't want this book to be too long. I will instead show you two pieces of writing that communicate the sort of distress I was in at my lowest. No-one else had read these words until I submitted this for publication. I am therefore less than 100% comfortable sharing them here. They are pretty raw but I include them because I believe that they convey the seriousness of the illness in a fairly concise, readable and human way. I also want to give stigma a dig in the ribs. And I believe that if you are suffering from severe depression at this moment in time, you will identify with these words.

Remember, skipping to chapter 3 from here might be a helpful strategy for you at this time. You decide what is good for you at this moment in time. You can always return later.

Both pieces of writing were entered into journals of mine at the time. I kept diaries of my thoughts and feelings on-and-off until about 2006. As I said in the introduction, I think doing so can be very therapeutic, but best done within a helpful CBT structure (see chapter 5 on thoughts - in particular thought records - which I started using from 2006 instead of a journal).

The first entry was written hastily on a morning in mid-June 1991 ; the second received more time and thought over about 2 weeks in 1997.

Age 21

I know that none of you will understand. All I can say is that I'm truly sorry, but I am no use living with my thoughts as they are. It is me that has destroyed myself, with my thoughts, and noone else's fault at all. It all stems from dad's death, and over the last 5 months my thoughts have snowballed into the meaningless-ness I experience today. I really want to be alive, but - you must understand - not thinking the way I do. If I could turn the clock back a year I would, but I can't. I'm so sorry, and I know a lot of you will be very confused and angry and sad. I have had a good life and done a lot of things in my 21 years - more than most. If there is a god I want to know - I can't wait to find out. Oh I am so confused, and you may look on me as very selfish, but I don't want it to be that way - try to understand - what I have written in here might help you understand a bit. Please

remember it's my thoughts that have destroyed me, not anyone else's, especially my family who I would love dearly to do well in life. I love you all. But that's it, I would love you all if anything meant anything to me anymore, but even that seems meaningless. Please do well without me and try not to dwell on my thoughts because noone could have changed them now - they are beyond the point of no return. I'm truly sorry............

The preamble to my only suicide attempt. On a beautiful, warm, sunny mid-summers morning back at home for the university holidays, I rose early so that mum couldn't see the look in my eyes. It was about 8 o'clock. I had been awake and petrified since about 4 in the morning. Mum knew I "wasn't right" : I had been quiet and withdrawn for the previous couple of weeks, reading lots of stuff on God and evolution, spending a lot of time in my bedroom, while avoiding golf and friends. It was almost a year since I had experienced depression for the first time in America. I was obsessed with finding answers to humankinds' existence, 'why are we here?', 'what is the point?', 'what is our purpose ?', "what does it all mean ?", "where / what is god ?" and so on ? I could not find the answers because I was looking for certainty, which of course does not exist in relation to these sorts of questions. I spoke timidly through my mum's bedroom door to tell her that I was going for a jog on the beach, and took a knife from the cutlery drawer in the kitchen. The stillness of that morning remains a vivid memory, as I jogged slowly, weak at the knees, towards the nearby beach. The bees and flies were buzzing around the marram grass as I made my way along the sand dunes, intermittently weeping. It was unusually warm and hazy for twenty past eight, but that meant absolutely nothing to me. I was distressed but determined to do it, to escape the torment. I found a hidden spot, a dip in the dunes, and, after plucking up the courage, started hacking at my wrist. It didn't hurt much. I was pretty numbed. I made a mess of my left wrist, did not sever any arteries, so I started on the right, then...... either the real me fought back a little bit, or the destructive side of me got tired. Whatever it was, it was just enough to get me to stop what I was doing. There was sand in my wounds. I went down to the waters-edge to rinse them out. I walked back up to the dunes and threw the (thankfully quite blunt) knife away into the middle of a thorn bush. I think I became resigned to living at that point. I stumbled along more dunes, then onto the golf course, clutching my sweatshirt over my arms to hide the mess. On the other side of the golf course I remember passing a delivery depot or a factory and some of the workers were outside for their break. They seemed to look at me but I'm not sure if they noticed that I was distressed. I eventually reached a phonebox some 5 miles along the coast in Irvine harbour and phoned 999. I sat hunched, waiting for the ambulance. It arrived, I got to hospital, and I was patched up..............

That was a close call. I hadn't really known what was wrong with me. I had previously been prescribed anti-depressants and told I was suffering from depression, but up until then it had not really registered. I had taken the pills only intermittently. That quote from William Styron springs to mind. To a large extent I thought I was right, there was no god, life was essentially meaningless, and therefore there was no point in living. Everyone else was blissfully ignorant, they all had it so wrong.

In the aftermath my mum and sisters rallied round. A close aunt caught the next train up to Scotland from Somerset to lend support. I was diagnosed by a psychiatrist with clinical depression. I believed her. Since then I've been on something of a quest to understand it more. Knowing that my enemy has a name, and that there is something known about it, has put me in a stronger position. I have since resisted the temptation to end my own life, despite being as ill as I was at 21.

I have endured quite a few serious depressive episodes or bouts* over the past 25 years or so, with many shorter, less serious episodes. Inbetween I have also lived well enough for most of the time. For example just a few weeks after the attempt I made on my own life I was well enough to join some mates on a trip to work as stewards at the British Open Golf Championship in Lytham St.Annes. I could have enjoyed it more, but I remember having a decent enough time. Like a well-adjusted sufferer of diabetes, asthma or other chronic condition, I get through the difficult spells and get on with living when I am feeling ok. There have been very difficult times for myself and my family, but I'm alive to tell the tale. Just. I again came close enough to write "farewell" notes when I was 27 and 34.

*Footnote * It is hard to objectively classify what an "episode" or "bout" is. Psychiatry has its own categorical systems, called DSM-V and ICD-10. These are huge manuals pigeon-holing human mental ill-health into separate classifications. They have a lot of* *positive uses including the provision of a useful framework to help us to understand the great complexity and variety involved in mental illness. But it is not a 100%* **valid or reliable** *system. For example, no psychiatric diagnosis can give an accurate prognosis for recovery (mainly because environmental factors generally play such a big part) ; and it is quite often the case (compared with general medicine) that one psychiatrist will diagnose someone with something while another will diagnose the same person with something else. Studies have actually shown that class can be a factor : a patient perceived as educated and middle-class has a higher chance of being diagnosed manic-depressive ; similarly, someone perceived as working-class and less educated is more likely to be diagnosed with a psychotic illness.*

Age 27

Believe me, from my point of view (and hopefully yours in the long run) my action is the lesser of two evils. The other option, to stumble on as I am, would be too humiliating for me and too much of a handicap and embarrassment for you. The memory of the healthy, reasonably jovial, decent bloke that I think I was would become far too distant if I limped on in limbo. You would start to resent me as much as I do. In a way I think the Barton males are 'cursed'. Probably not in a spiritual way - probably more in a genetic sense. It is best for the line to cease at me. God forbid that I struggle on, make some sort of temporary recovery, meet a girl willing to take a chance with me, get married, have kids and then relapse. I cannot risk the chance of that happening. Imagine having a dad like me when I'm in this sorry state. Some role model I'd be. F**k that.

You couldn't have done anymore, and you couldn't have prevented it. I have planned it thoroughly and quietly and made sure I dropped no hints. I love you all a great deal. I know this is an unusual way to show it, but I just couldn't go on as a pathetic excuse for a man that I am. Life, despite our welfare state, NHS, safety net structures, is essentially about survival of the fittest / extinction of the unfit. The country cannot afford burdens like me. I simply seem to be weak, and I have too much pride to continue on as a drain on the family finances and the taxpayer. Christ, if I'd lived in Nazi Germany I'd have been exterminated years ago. I so much want to contribute to society but I don't have the reserves in me to beat this torture and do so. I can console myself in the thought that at least I have the balls to do this ; I have the sense of self-sufficiency required to know when it is time to stop leaning on others and call it a day. Try to think of me as a shamed Samurai warrior, leaning on to his sword for an honourable exit.

If you are honest with yourselves you will have to admit that there is probably a little sense of relief deep within you. Don't feel guilty about this. If the roles were reversed I am sure I would feel absolutely devastated to start with (because of my love for you) but hopefully in time I would realise that my sister or mother was becoming a bit of a burden and embarrassment, and that at least they were now at peace and out of their misery. The positive to draw from this is that I am now at peace and fulfilling a useful function (fertilising the grass - can you sprinkle my ashes on the 2nd hole at Bushfoot - I have so many happy memories of golfing there), and you are now all free to get on with your lives and fulfil your potential.

This is me being very selfish. I don't deny that. I know you will be confused, numb, angry, sad, bitter, regretful......... if I was even a reasonably whole person and one of you did this I would be all of those things and more. Just remember that this is the depressive illness killing me. Just like heart disease kills some and cancer kills others. I have been driven to this by the turmoil inside my head and the general numbness of my body. I am lucky to have got this far in life - 6 years ago I was serious but despite hacking at myself the knife was too blunt and I ran out of energy (you can tell the doctor that - I always had the feeling that she thought it was just an attention-seeking cry for help).

I am sincerely sorry for leaving you with my debts (see separate sheet). My reckoning is that I am cutting your losses by opting out now. I HATE being a burden, physically, emotionally and economically. I can't stress that enough. I recognise that from your point of view I may not be as much of a hassle as I feel I am, but that is not really the point. The primary issue of importance here is that I am 27 and still a boy. I can't seem to survive in the thick of life. My feelings of self-loathing have reached hitherto unprecedented levels. The shame I feel when I scuttle around the town for the simplest of messages, averse to eye-contact and conversation ; when I don't have the backbone to give my sister a hand carrying crates of bottles from the

Spar, cowering in the car instead ; when I have to leave my mother to challenge the gasman for signing us up on a dodgy deal, standing hunched and big-nosed nearby, knowing what to say a second after it should have been said, too scared to say anything anyway, and paranoid about the gasman thinking I'm a woose of immense proportions with no cohones whatsoever. My thoughts are simply too distressing this time.

I also HATE being constantly pre-occupied with myself. But I just can't help it. That is why, from my point of view, I am doing this for you in a way, because you will be rid of the introspective, arm-folding, self-self-self obsessed Bobby Bachelor the potentially bloated lithium-popping baldy. It saddens me alot to leave you, because the healthy part of me wants to live. I will be crying when I finally go because I will miss you all terribly - you are such a wonderful family and I hope and pray you can get on with your lives once you have come to terms with what I've done. I hope this letter helps you to understand that suicide is not always a completely selfish, impulsive, irrational act (I would be grateful if you could photocopy this and pass it round at the funeral). It's just that this healthy part of me is so weak now, so over-run and riddled with mental illness, that I can't fight any longer. I have tried my utmost, I think you know that. Exercise, diet, meditation, herbs, positive thinking, dismissal of negative thoughts, challenging of negative thoughts, anti-depressants, counselling, detoxification, forgiving my father, grief exploration, wacky therapies (of which, sleeping with 2 tennis balls in a sock under my head probably takes the biscuit)............ every avenue bar a witch doctor has been explored, but to no avail.

Mum, I know you will be especially distressed when you realise what I've done. Again, I hope that by reading this you will gain at least a little understanding and comfort. I can't stress the following enough - YOU ARE NOT TO BLAME IN ANY WAY, YOU ARE A GENUINELY GOOD PERSON AND A LOVING, CARING AND VERY CAPABLE MOTHER. THERE IS NOTHING MORE YOU COULD HAVE DONE FOR ME. To be honest, if it had not been for yourself and my sisters (plus other family and friends, but primarily you three), I would not have survived this long. I would have been dead years ago. I mean that. You have all been so patient and supportive. You must have had to bite your tongue so many times, because no matter what people say, the natural instinct with someone in my condition is to tell them to bloody well get a grip and pull themselves together.

You'll no doubt discuss this till you're blue in the face. For what its worth, I don't know why I moved from being headboy with sporting and academic promise to under-achieving twenty something with chemical imbalance. Maybe I didn't grieve enough over losing my father - my best friend. Maybe it was his confusing alcoholic behaviour in my teenage years which sewed the seeds. Maybe it was simply a genetic weakness I inherited from somewhere in the family, something that would have reared its ugly head even if dad had still been alive and well, and everything in the family was hunky-dory. Most likely it was some combination of these. Whatever, it basically boils down to being nobody's fault (except maybe dad's, and I intend to quiz him about it, don't you worry). NONE OF YOU ARE TO BLAME.

I'm glad that I've managed to contribute a little since coming home. Painting, putting up shelves, organising the home files, walking the dog......... I suppose I haven't been completely useless. But we've run out of wee jobs for me to do.

I don't have a great deal. Divide it between yourselves amicably. Give my golf clubs to a deserving junior at the club and my putter back to Auntie Audrey.

Maybe I'll get another chance in my next life. I know that my healthy self would have made a good husband and father. But it is not to be. Mum, you're a great believer in fate, so it must be that someone or something, somewhere, is calling me to come in, my time is up. Look on it as I'm being substituted early from the game of life. My performance has not been up to scratch. I look forward to seeing you all after the game on the other side (I do hope it's not "lights out"). Rest assured, if I can manage it, those of you whom I love and respect will receive my utmost efforts to positively influence your games from the bench. The few I have no respect for will be getting pelters........

And there it ended. (by the way, in case you're not au fait with Glaswegian slang, "pelters" equates to verbal abuse). I was teetering on the brink. It had taken me over a week to write and revise but I didn't finish it off. I started to feel a bit better soon after. Nowhere near back to normal, but my hope levels rose that notch or two required to see some sort of future. A faint light at the end of a long tunnel. And I did go on to get properly better (with the help of others, beneficial medication, and an assertive skills therapy group at a local Mental Health Day Unit).

Some of the above is so negative, so extreme and so full of self-hatred that it's almost amusing - in a very dark sort of way - for me to read parts of it now (my nose is probably above average but not actually that big, I haven't gone bald (yet !) and, at the time of writing this, I'm not excessively overweight). But it was far from funny at the time. I was trying my very utmost to explain my actions so as to lessen the hurt for those left behind. Thankfully I clung on. When I look back at this distressed and negative note, I am struck by one other particular thing ; the persuasive cunning of this illness to push you to the brink of carrying out the most final of acts of self-loathing. It can become so tempting to go along with it.

I am so grateful to have clung on. I went on to meet my wife-to-be at 32 and get married at 35. We are very fortunate to have a solid, close and loving partnership together. We also have a wonderful daughter who I hope will benefit from reading this when she is old enough. I am, I think, a decent husband and father. My sisters have married and altogether I have nine lovely nephews and nieces. Being married and becoming a father has not completely immunised me from depression, but it has certainly helped my self-esteem and matured my personality. I get ill less now, for less time.

Age 34

The farewell note aged 34 after stopping my medications was in essence pretty similar to this, covering the same themes. The acidic self-hatred, the shame, the inadequacy, the illogical analogies, the apologising, the odd bit of dark humour, the pleas for forgiveness, the irrational attempts to rationalise my intended actions, the reassurances that noone could have prevented me, the promises that I'll try and repay loved ones from heaven, and the hypothesising on the reasons behind my state of mind. The only essential difference was that I had a little bit of money to leave behind at 34. I felt 'better' that at least I wasn't leaving a pile of debts.

With this episode lasting 3 tortuous months, I tried all sorts to get well again. Most of the stuff I mentioned aged 27. Plus I remember twice a day doing headstands in order to try to get more blood to flow to my brain. I don't think that was much use. But at least I wasn't staring at the 4 walls (well I suppose I was, only upside down!). Joking aside, the act of doing a head stand may or may not have helped improve my brain function, but regardless, at least I was being constructive and active instead of inert and passive.

As time dragged on I consciously decided to also write down the "case for the defence". That is, I tried to argue against the strong, compelling case my depressive side was making for killing myself. But I still felt I was losing the battle. I had formulated a pretty solid plan of how I would end it, **but importantly, I didn't do anything impulsively.** I gave it a little time and my mood started to lift again. I hit rock-bottom and held on. Unlike my father, I persevered. I have been ill since then, but I have never seriously contemplated taking my life again. I have too much to live for.

The Only Way is Up

So, basically, once you've survived the worst, the only way is up. At this moment you may be on the way down and still have the worst to come, or you may be on the way back up, experiencing occasional setbacks. **But you will get there in the end.**

Be aware that some of the worries and insecurities you experienced at different points on the way down, may re-emerge on the way back up. As you move up through the levels of recovery you can encounter similar thoughts and feelings that haunted you on the descent. Almost in a mirror-image sort of a way. It is as if depression is clinging to you like pond weed, trying to pull you back down again. Sometimes depression wins temporarily and you have to work to free yourself all over again. But as your recovery gains momentum, hopefully you feel stronger and more able to deal with the negative thoughts. You can pull your legs clear of the weed with more conviction.

It is also worth saying that it is probably best not to react immediately to the whirl of emotions you may experience as you recover. Be patient for a little while longer and give things time to settle. If you can, postpone any big decisions in your life.

As Dr. Jon Allen described so well in chapter 1, recovery can take a long time and be extremely difficult. But if you persuade yourself to remain patient, and work at those "leverage areas", you at least have a chance of getting back to good health. Which, to put it bluntly, is more than you have if you're dead.

Here is a great example of perseverance. The popular entertainer and comedian Spike Milligan was one person who hung on for dear life during many depressive episodes. During one of his worst, which lasted for over a year between 1990 and 1991, he was close to calling it a day. He was treated in hospital with medication, counselling and Electroconvulsive Therapy (ECT), all seemingly to no avail. Then, about one month before Christmas 1991, the depression lifted as suddenly and as inexplicably as it had originally struck. He got back to his usual, humorous, outgoing and enthusiastic self again. There is a very funny clip of him on YouTube receiving a lifetime achievement award in 1994. He went on to live until 2002. I'm sure he wasn't on top form all that time, but I'm equally as sure he died thinking he was glad to have made it to 83.

Different Approaches

The remainder of the book will now be devoted to practical ways of managing your mental-physical illness.

There are two broad approaches to tackling this illness. Based on the reductionist viewpoint that all matter can be studied at the micro-level, we will first look at **bottom-up solutions.** That is, treating the condition at the cellular level upwards, with medication (chapter 3) and good nutrition (chapter 4).

Then, from chapter 5, we will look at the **top-down approach.** That is, solutions from the spiritual to the emotional, psychological and physical that help to **heal from the top-down.**

By employing a combination of both approaches I predict that you will ultimately get better and stay better for longer periods of time.
Before the next chapter on medications, let me stress again that it is up to you which of the following you have a go at. There will be options I suggest which you will dismiss straight away. But there will be others you can try. You may be doing some, or a lot of them already. If so, that's great. You may also be occupying your time with other positive non-threatening activities not mentioned here. Even better.

A word of warning. Be wary of your depressive side trying to sabotage you. It will do its utmost to undermine your efforts. Try to distinguish between **YOU** assessing the worth of a potential activity and **IT** dismissing an activity because .... *you're ill, you're weak, you're weird, there's no point, what will others think ? , you can't win, you should be ashamed of yourself, you don't need that................* and all sorts of insidious, tempting lines of thought.

Tell yourself this assertively, repeat it (or your own variation of it) from this point forward, no matter how weak you feel :

" **I am in charge here depression, you can protest all you want, I hear what you are saying, but I choose not to believe it.
I will engage in non-threatening constructive activity because it's good for me, the HEALTHY ME.
I will choose constructive activity I can cope with, over inertia and rumination. Eventually, although I'm not sure when, I will SUCCEED, get better, and be a stronger person for it.**"

As you say this, depression will still be there, omni-present, lurking in the wings, or on stage trying to distract you or shut you up. It does that alot.

Be patient, be brave, and remember, although you may feel out of control at the moment, your pilot light is not out, it is merely dimmed. Ultimately the fire in your belly will return, you are in charge, and you will recover.

Bottom-Up

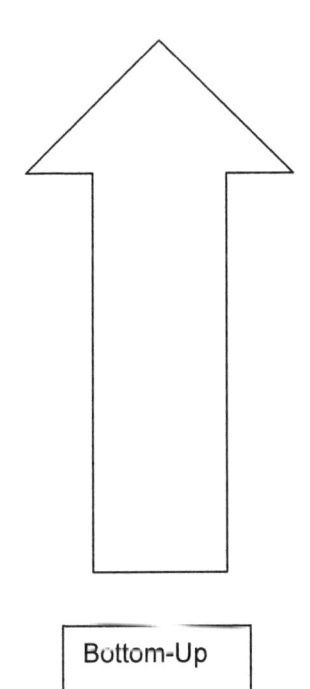

Chapter 3 : Clinical Depression, Medications & Supplements

We start with medication - ahead of diet, the cognitive therapies and other behavioural strategies - because it is a very important piece of the jigsaw. It is often the most important factor involved in recovery from clinical depression (remember we are talking about moderate-to-severe depression here, not mild...... the latter can often be endured without resort to medication). It certainly has been for me.

My lengthy 2003 - 2004 relapse at age 34 was largely precipitated by an attempt to come off my prescribed medication. At the time this was lithium carbonate (a mood-stabiliser) and citalopram (an SSRI anti-depressant). The combination of lithium plus an anti-depressant has been shown to help prevent or minimise the recurrence of depressive illness. I had been concerned that the "doctor's bible" (the British National Formulary or BNF) recommends that lithium should only be taken for 3-5 years, "unless benefit persists." I had been taking it for about 5½. These were relatively symptom and side-effect free years (ie the benefit was persisting). Life was not perfect : I had had a couple of short relapses triggered by stressful life events, but where previously I might have been submerged for a month or more, these only lasted for about a week each.

The risks of long-term lithium use include danger of damage to the liver, kidneys and thyroid. I was worried about this and also wanted to see if the illness had "burnt itself out". In addition, a part of me wanted to see if I could "be a man" and survive without the crutch of medication. And, although there was no pressure from my future wife, trying to "prove something" to her was in the mix too (we had only been going out for a few months at this time). I knew that I was taking a big risk, but I also knew that if it didn't work out, it would not be a disaster to resume taking the pills.

It seemed a good time to try. I was back in Scotland near my family, had good support around me, a flat of my own, and a secure job which I enjoyed. I did it the recommended way, discussing it with a Consultant Psychiatrist in July 2003, informing my GP and withdrawing gradually. The citalopram was tapered off first, over about 4 weeks. I waited 3 months then tried to cut back on the lithium. Shortly after cutting back by a quarter, I relapsed. Looking back, it had been on the cards : symptoms had been slowly but surely creeping back into my system. Among other things I became preoccupied with my past again. I became overly-sensitive with friends about issues I would usually have laughed off or coped with more assertively. I struggled to focus on the here-and-now. On the 19 December 2003, on the way to what I perceived might turn out to be a stressful social engagement, I crossed back over the "blurred boundaries of the normal range of mood" into illness. Various other factors were involved but the meds were absolutely crucial. It is too much of a coincidence that I did well - indeed at times did very well, despite life's usual unavoidable stresses - for 5½ years on this medication ; and within 4 months of reducing them I was back in the depths of despair.

On 21 December 2003 I started back on the original doses of the two medicines. It took a heck of a long while (about 12 weeks off work), but eventually I got better again.

So I have good reason to believe that clinical depression is at least partly a physical illness, requiring pharmacological intervention. This is in agreement with generally accepted medical opinion ; indeed recent evidence is even pointing to clinical depression being an inflammatory illness. Based on reviews of all the best literature and research, doctors recommend that moderate-to-severe depression is best treated with a combination of medication, diet, non-threatening activity and talking therapy.

Dr. Jon Allen of the "Catch 22" article also talks of there being "good reason" for us to think of depression as both a mental **and physical illness** :

1. Depression can be partly due to genetic (inherited) vulnerability. A recent large-scale genetic study from Massachusetts General Hospital (Craig Hyde and colleagues) has identified 15 different regions on the genome that are associated with depression in individuals of European ancestry. I think it is safe to assume that there are also vulnerability genes in people of non-European heritage.
2. The risk of developing depression is increased by stressful early life experience, which can lead to changes in brain

chemistry. These changes probably prime the vulnerability genes and render them more likely to be switched on.
3. It is associated with changes in patterns of brain functioning (a reduction in blood supply to the front of the brain being one).
4. It is often accompanied by physical ill-health.
5. It is responsive to medications and, as last resorts, repeated transcranial magnetic stimulation (rTMS) or electro-convulsive therapy (ECT). See ch.7 for more detail.

Most of you reading this book will know what you are suffering from, but there's a chance that some of you will be unsure what is wrong. If that is you, I hope this book helps to reassure you that you are not going mad, nor are you a terrible person. Clinical Depression envelops almost every aspect of a person's life. It is a most complex biological disorder of the brain precisely because individual psychology, biology, social circumstances and spiritual beliefs are so important too.

But what exactly are the symptoms? I have mentioned most of them in passing, in the introduction and in chapters 1 and 2, but it is well worth listing them comprehensively here, in condensed form.

Core physical symptoms (you may have some or all of these) :

- Loss of energy.
- Loss of interest in usual activities, poor motivation.
- Feeling physically ill / run down.
- Poor concentration.
- Altered appetite (usually decreased, but sometimes increased).
- Altered sleep (usually insomnia and early morning wakening, but sometimes oversleeping). For those affected by early morning wakening, time of awakening can be a rough indicator of severity of the illness. At my worst I routinely wake up as early as 0300, while a milder episode involves waking sometime around 0600.
- Reduced sex drive / libido.
- Physical and mental sluggishness, a feeling of being very slowed up.

- Psychomotor agitation (pacing, wringing hands or folding arms alot) or retardation (lying around or being unable to move without effort).
- An overall feeling of "numbness", inadequacy and self-loathing (depression is after all primarily a disorder of affect or feeling), which renders the person more exposed to negative, unhelpful thoughts they would usually deal with quite effectively. Interestingly if you pay close attention you will probably notice that the "core you" still occasionally thinks helpful, positive thoughts at times, but they do not lead to any corresponding positive emotion.

Other physical symptoms that may be present :

- Heartburn
- Indigestion
- Constipation
- Stomach ulcers
- Dry skin, hair and mouth
- Pins and needles
- Unusual pains
- Headaches
- Altered periods

Core psychological symptoms (again, you may have some or all of these) :

- Hopelessness
- Feelings of helplessness
- Meaninglessness
- Apathy / withdrawl / avoidance
- Indecision
- Clumsiness and absent-mindedness
- Confusion
- Lowered self-esteem
- Inappropriate guilt and self-blame
- Ruminating about past events / mistakes
- Anxiety / panic / obsessional worry

- Increased dreaming
- Paranoid thoughts
- Suicidal thoughts ; ideas ; a vague intent ; or a fully-fledged plan to take your own life

Whatever combination of symptoms you have, if you are severely depressed your level of functioning will be significantly impaired. Psychiatric definitions of depression stipulate that you should have some or all of these symptoms for most of the day every day for 2 weeks before a diagnosis can be made. I disagree with that. Certainly at times my experience has been that spells of severe depression can last less than 2 weeks. It is the lowering of your mood that counts, not how long it lasts.

(It is also worth noting that a lot of these symptoms can be present in other disorders, such as low thyroid functioning, and that depressive symptoms can also be brought on by taking some medications eg steroids. In partnership with your GP you should eliminate possible physical causes before a definitive diagnosis of depression is made.)

It could be argued that you could put up with the physical symptoms on their own, but throw in the psychological, social and spiritual symptoms and it becomes very, **very difficult (but not impossible)**. Many people who have endured severe clinical depression will say that the psychic pain of the illness is worse than any physical pain they have experienced (again this justifies the "£44,237 compared with £5,556" distinction discussed in chapter 1).

So those are the symptoms. But how does depressive illness normally take its course? Can it be compared to any other illness?

A Clear, Helpful Model for Depression : The Ulcer Model

In his very readable book "Psychiatric Drugs Explained", Professor David Healy of Bangor University in Wales makes many points that stress the importance of medication in treating major depression. He also draws a really useful analogy between a physical illness (stomach ulcers) and depression. It's not a perfect one. He acknowledges that it simplifies both depression and ulcers. But it helps to illustrate the main features of depression, including the role for medication.

- Ulcers usually come on after a stressful period. Depression is similar. Ulcers don't automatically clear up once the stress has stopped. They are therefore both a psychological and physical problem. Likewise, depression is not just "in your head" and can persist for weeks and months once the stress subsides. It's like the circuitry in your brain buckles under stress and takes a while to reboot itself.

- Ulcers are appropriately treated with drugs. Depression also responds to medication (most of the time, and as you will see in chapter 8, the situation with more personalised medication looks set to improve response rates to antidepressants).

- Ulcers are initially unaffected by anti-ulcer drugs. The pain continues and there seems to be little improvement. However, after a week or two, the pain of the ulcer begins to fade as the wound closes over. As the pain goes, the anxiety associated with having an ulcer also goes. Similarly, anti-depressants work slowly to heal the underlying depression. As the pain of the depression subsides, so feelings of anxiety, hopelessness, guilt and self-hatred retreat.

- Anxious people who don't have an ulcer don't benefit from ulcer drugs. Likewise, anti-depressants are of little use in sad and unhappy people if they don't have the 'brain ulcer' of clinical depression.

- Current research suggests that it is wise to remain on an anti-ulcer drug for at least 3-6 months after the ulcer has closed, in case the ulcer reopens. Sometimes ongoing ulcer medication is recommended to those vulnerable to ulcers. This is roughly the same advice given to people on anti-depressants, in case the depression recurs (actually it is closer to the 6 months). For people who have had a number of depressive episodes it is often prudent to opt for permanent, preventative on-going treatment.

- If an ulcer is not too severe it is often possible to treat it without medication. Lifestyle and diet changes can suffice. For example

: eating little and often throughout the day ; avoiding hot, spicy food ; avoiding or cutting down on smoking and alcohol ; and relaxing. So it is with mild depression. Lifestyle and diet changes (see chapters 4 - 6) combined with a "talking therapy" can promote recovery on their own.

- Serious ulcers can resolve without medication, but this presents a severe test for the body. A major depressive episode will also usually eventually lift of its own accord, but this presents a huge challenge to anyone contemplating trying to survive without medication. If you find yourself in this position, struggling on without medication, perhaps you could reconsider.

- Importantly, ulcers normally clear up more quickly and effectively when the patient follows lifestyle and diet changes AND takes an anti-ulcer medication. In the same way, people with severe clinical depression are likely to make a quicker recovery if they combine an anti-depressant with non-threatening activity, thought-challenging, a balanced, therapeutic diet, and the help of trusted friends / family / therapist.

- Some people have ulcer problems which recur frequently. This appears to be associated with the presence of an organism in the gut, helicobacter pylori. Some people are also vulnerable to recurrent depressive episodes. This may also be down to a predisposing factor, possibly a chemical imbalance in the brain brought about by stressful early life experiences. And possibly combined with a genetic vulnerability. At present, the research is unclear as to the exact nature of this. Interestingly there is some fascinating work on gut flora possibly influencing our mood (see chapters 4 and 8). This seems rather bizarre but the science is developing on this one. Certainly it is clear that certain types of people benefit from permanent ongoing treatment to help prevent relapse.

All in all, arguably a very useful and hopeful comparison. Especially for someone in the throes of the illness who may be struggling to take information on board. I certainly find it useful. And potentially helpful for friends and relatives who find it difficult to grasp the nature of severe clinical depression.

Climate and Weather

Sticking with the analogy / metaphor theme, Healy also draws on meteorological terminology.

He considers the terms 'mood' and 'emotion'. He likens our moods to the climate, and our emotions to the weather. He argues that **severe clinical depression is like a change in the climate, rather than simply a change in the weather.** Anti-depressants work to reset climate (mood) parameters rather than act on a particular piece of bad weather (emotions). This helps to explain why it takes so long for antidepressants to work. Like it takes a while to turn a supercontainer ship around, it takes a while for reset climate controls to feed through to the weather on the ground. If severe depression was simply an emotional and/or psychological problem, people could talk their way out of it somehow, but that is patently not the case if you are locked in the prison of the illness.

Depression is like a part of the brain "blowing a fuse"

Dr Tim Cantopher puts forward a helpful idea in his book "Depression : The Curse of the Strong". Like Jon Allen in chapter 1 he also describes clinical depression as more of a physical illness and likens the effect on our emotional regulation centre (the limbic system of the brain) to the "blowing of a fuse". He suggests that some people (the ones who tend to bend over backwards for others) are more vulnerable than others, and draws the analogy between our limbic system and different values of fuses (eg 3A, 5A, 13A), which are designed as sacrificial devices to be able to withstand different peaks of electricity current. He argues that people who are vulnerable to depression are fitted with limbic systems akin to a 3 or 5 amp fuse, which blow or melt at relatively low levels of current, or stress. More resilient individuals (in terms of depression) may possess the equivalent of 13 amp fuses, rendering them more immune to stress.

Like we are doing here, he emphasises that people do recover from depression with patience and persistence and can stay well if they make helpful decisions. The blown fuse can be replaced / recover, and last a long time if not subjected to excessive stress.

What do anti-depressants actually do?

Quite simply, psychiatry isn't quite sure exactly how the anti-depressants work. This is not so much of a surprise when you consider how complex our brains are. But they do act on the brain is unique ways :

1) Unlike other psychoactive substances such as caffeine, nicotine, alcohol, marijuana and the tranquilisers, antidepressants do not act immediately on the brain. It takes about 30 minutes for side-effects to become apparent. Generally these will be mild. In fact it is often hard to distinguish between symptoms of the illness and side-effects of the medication. That said, the most common side-effects are dry mouth, sedation and headache (more will be said on this later in the chapter).

2) They typically take 2 - 6 weeks to help to lift the clinical depression (heal the "brain ulcer"). Sometimes longer. Interestingly, they only seem to do something positive for people who are depressed. **They do not make the non-depressed any happier.** They are not happy-clappy stimulants. Contrast this with stimulants such as caffeine, cocaine and amphetamines, which all have roughly the same physical effect on whoever takes them, no matter what their mood.

3) Depending on the specific medication, the anti-depressants generally act on the mood-related neurotransmitters, noradrenaline (N) and serotonin (S). The anti-depressants help to prevent reuptake of these chemicals in the gap between brain cells (neurones). More specifically, when information is being communicated between neurones, N and S are the chemical messengers released at the synapse, into the gap between neurones. The amount of N and S tends to be lower in the depressed person's brain. Levels are more easily depleted. Less N and S are being released at the synapses. The anti-depressants seem to stop the brain's natural tendency to "sweep up" left-over N and S once it is between the cells, thereby prolonging their effect on the synapse and helping to lift mood (see figure 2 overleaf).

Figure 2 : The action of antidepressants on the neurones of the brain.

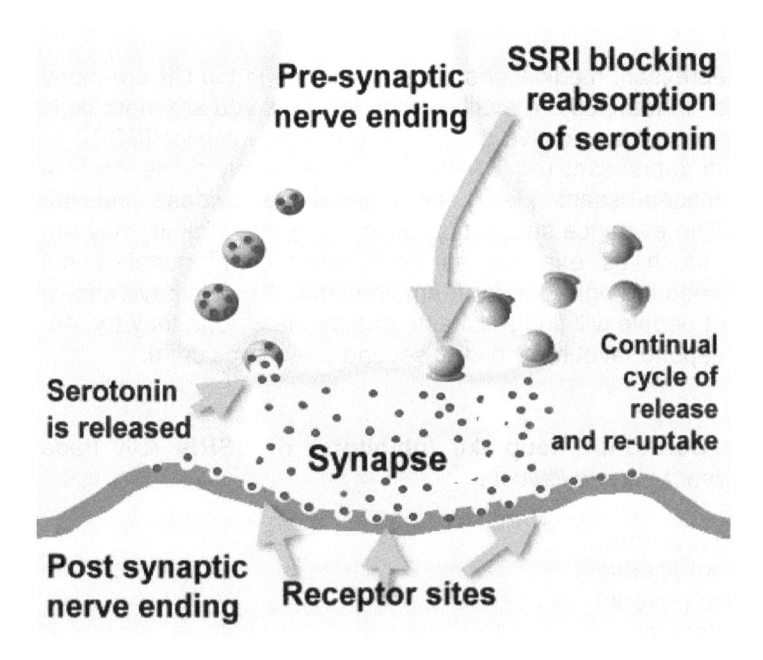

Pre-synaptic nerve ending

SSRI blocking reabsorption of serotonin

Serotonin is released

Synapse

Continual cycle of release and re-uptake

Post synaptic nerve ending **Receptor sites**

This applies equally to noradrenaline (from www.alanpriest.f2s.com)

4) They are not addictive in the way the benzodiazepines are [eg : *(trade names in brackets and italics)* diazepam *(valium)* ; nitrazepam *(mogadon)* ; and lorazepam *(ativan)*], but some are dangerous in overdose (the older tricyclics – see below).

In the context of this book I do not want to say a lot more about what the anti-depressants do. There are many books out there that can enlighten you further should you want to find out more. The fact is that, providing you are put on the right type for you (which can involve trial and error), they can help, and the side-effects are generally minimal or manageable. Your "climate" is readjusted, your "ulcer heals itself", your "blown fuse is replaced" and your "weather" eventually improves.

Specific Antidepressants :

Which are most often prescribed?

The antidepressant medications licensed for use in the UK are many and varied. In total, 26 are available. At this time you are most likely to be prescribed a selective serotonin re-uptake inhibitor (SSRI) or related anti-depressant (eg SNRIs) ; or more rarely these days, a tricyclic antidepressant (TAD) or monoamine oxidase inhibitor (MAOL). The evidence shows that once (or if) they kick in, they are all pretty much as effective as each other. Unfortunately not everyone finds the right one for them first time. Studies have shown that 95% of people will find a suitable one by the 6th one they try, 40-60% will respond favourably by the second one (drugs.com).

Common Serotonin Reuptake Inhibitors, or SSRIs *(UK trade names in brackets and italics)* :

citalopram *(cipramil)*
escitalopram *(cipralex)*
fluvoxamine *(faverin)*
fluoxetine *(prozac)*
paroxetine *(seroxat)*
sertraline *(lustral)*
duloxetine *(cymbalta)*
venlafaxine *(efexor)*, technically a serotonin **and** noradrenaline reuptake inhibitor (SNRI).

This is not an exhaustive list [see www.mind.org.uk/antidepressants A-Z or the British National Formulary (BNF) for such a list]. The SSRI's have been available from the mid-1980's. They are taken in various doses. They are relatively low on side-effects and are safest (but not completely safe) in overdose. They can help with associated anxiety and are not generally sedating. Like the related tricyclics, they also have few anti-muscarinic side-effects (eg dry mouth, thirst, dry skin). However, they do have side-effects of their own, such as the possibility of sexual dysfunction, insomnia, nausea and vomiting. (the list of possible side-effects is almost endless. See psychiatric text books, the BNF, or your own doctor if you want to find out more).

(It is worth stressing the word **possible** beside the word **side-effects**, because often patients experience very few or no side-effects at all. Also, some may experience uncomfortable side-effects to start with, which then subside completely as time goes on. Earlier in my career I worked in a Clinical Research Organisation where clinical trials of new medications are conducted, and even if only 1 in 10,000 people report a possible side-effect, it is added to the medication info sheet.

Withdrawl from an SSRI is sometimes more problematic compared with the older tricyclics. It needs to be done slowly to avoid symptoms such as headache, nausea, dizziness and anxiety. Again, always consult your doctor and err on the side of going slowly.

Tricyclic Antidepressants

Prescribed medications included here are *(UK trade names in brackets and italics)* :

amitryptaline *(tryptizol / lentizol)*
clomipramine *(anafranil)*
dothiepin *(prothiaden)*
doxepin *(sinequan)*
*imipramine *(tofranil)*
*lofepramine *(gamanil)*
norpramine *(norpramin)*
*nortriptyline *(allegron / motival / motipress)*
*protriptyline *(concordin)*
**trimipramine *(surmontil)*
* less sedating
** more sedating

The older tricyclics are usually taken in doses of 75 - 150 mg a day, but this can vary depending on the severity of your symptoms. They usually help to improve sleep and appetite (some are more sedating than others), and lessen associated anxiety. This can happen almost immediately. But, like all the anti-depressants, mood will generally not lift for at least 2 weeks. Side-effects such as cardiac arrythmias, low blood pressure, dry mouth, constipation, sweating, dizziness and headache (antimuscarinic side-effects) are all possible. They are not addictive and are not known to become any less effective over time.

Despite being as effective as the newer SSRI's, the tricyclics are not as popular as they used to be, because in overdose they are more cardiotoxic, pro-convulsive and generally life-threatening (97% of all single anti-depressant overdose deaths are due to tricyclics ; about 300 deaths a year in the UK). Doctors are therefore often less keen to prescribe an older-type tricyclic to someone with clinical depression.

Antidepressants related to the tricyclics *(UK trade names in brackets and italics)* :

Amoxapine *(asendis)*
maprotiline *(ludiomil)*
mianserin *(norval)*
mirtazepine *(zispin)*
nefazodone *(dutonin)*
trazodone *(molipaxin)*

The advantage of these related drugs is that they cause less antimuscarinic side-effects, including a lower likelihood of sexual dysfunction (the SSRI's and tricyclics can cause problems with reduced sensation and delayed orgasm - so much so that the SSRI's are sometimes prescribed for premature ejaculation). They also tend to be less dangerous to the heart and less dangerous in overdose. But they retain the often therapeutic sedating effect.

However, as with a lot in psychiatry, it is worth stressing that every patient is an individual, and an older tricyclic might just happen to suit one person more than one of the related drugs or an SSRI. You may have to go through a trial-and-error phase before you become established on the right one for you. As said, the commonly prescribed ones are usually pretty much as effective as each other, but one may cause you less side-effects than another. Put simply, prescribing in psychiatry is often as much an art as it is a science (though that may be set to change – see chapter 8).

Mono-amine Oxidase Inhibitors, or MAOL's *(trade names in brackets and italics)* :

phenelzine *(nardil)*
moclebomide *(manerix)* less severe potential side-effects.
Isocarboxazid *(marplan)*
tranylcypromine *(parstelin)*

These drugs are used very rarely now. They are mildly stimulant and most often tried when other anti-depressants have proved unsuccessful. This is because there are dangers from drug and dietary interactions when taking an MAOL. In particular, patients have to avoid most cheeses, avocados, bananas, herring, liver, smoked sausage, and red wine. How much they have to avoid these and other foods depends on the individual MAOL in question. Regarding drug interactions, there needs to be a specified break before a patient stops another treatment and starts an MAOL. Likewise, if a patient stops an MAOL they must wait before starting something else. So, if at all possible, your doctor will be unlikely to suggest one of these medications

Lithium Carbonate

Lithium Carbonate *(Priadel)* is best-known as a treatment for bipolar illness (formerly known as manic-depression). But if you suffer from recurrent depressive illness your doctor might suggest (or you might suggest to your doctor) that lithium be added alongside your anti-depressant as a preventative treatment. This would be ongoing treatment.

There is good evidence indicating a role for lithium in recurrent major depression. It has been used widely for 60 years and it is the only mood stabiliser with proven anti-suicide effects (I can vouch for this). The currently accepted wisdom is that if you have had 2 episodes in one year, or 3 episodes over the course of 2 years, you may benefit from the addition of lithium, or lithium augmentation.

There are slight inconveniences to lifestyle. Regular blood samples have to be taken in order to check lithium levels, liver, kidney and thyroid function. Once stabilised on the drug, this is usually every 6 months and sometimes annually. To help prevent relapse, doctors generally like to aim for a therapeutic blood level of between 0.4mmol/l and 0.8mmol/l. There is also the chance of side-effects like fine tremor, thirst, urinary frequency and others. It is important to drink consistently adequate amounts of fluids (1.5-2 litres per day) and regulate sodium intake, as blood lithium levels can rise if a person becomes dehydrated. If someone proves unresponsive to lithium, there may be a role for another mood-stabiliser, carbamazepine.

I started taking lithium in 1998, aged 28. After 18 years the only noticeable side-effect I experience is the fine tremor, which I consider a very small price to pay for generally stable mental health.

"Over-the-Counter" Medications and Supplements

St. Johns Wort (Hypericum Perforatum)

If you are wary of, or cannot be persuaded of the merits of orthodox psychiatry, this natural herbal anti-depressant may be of interest to you. It is known by some as the 'sunshine herb', because of its yellow flowers. Used widely in Germany, it seems to work in a similar way to the SSRI's. In clinical trials, 800 mg per day was shown to be equivalent to a low-dose 20mg per day fluoxetine in mild to moderate depression. However, the research generally points to less efficacy in severe depression.

In its favour, side-effects are generally similar to the other anti-depressants, and mostly mild. The only exception is a rare, but potentially uncomfortable, increased sunburn risk. If you want to take St. John's Wort it is advisable to talk with your GP, as there are quite a few other medications which may interact negatively with it eg warfarin, some anticonvulsants and the oral contraceptive.

Omega 3 Fatty Acids

One of the most popular dietary myths of the last 40 years has been that fats (or lipids) are bad for you. This is true to an extent. Most of us know that eating a lot of saturated fats increases our risk of heart disease. If you smoke and don't exercise, your risk increases again. But, not all fats are bad news. The **essential polyunsaturated fats - omega-3 and omega-6 - are necessary for optimal health.** Omega-3's are obtained from oily fish, but also from wild game meat, flaxseed oil, leafy green vegetables, and walnuts. Omega-6's are found mainly in vegetable and seed oils, which are very prominent in the typical western diet. In fact, it is estimated that most of us currently eat omega-6 fatty acids to omega-3's in a ratio of 10 or 20-to-1. Significantly, the emerging evidence is that we should ideally aim for a 'yin-yang' balance between the two, in the order of 1-to-1.

In his book "The Omega-3 Connection", Dr. Andrew Stoll of Harvard Medical School puts forward a strong series of arguments for increasing our consumption of omega 3 fatty acids. He reminds us that the cardiovascular and general health benefits of the omega-3 fatty acids have been known for a while now. Eating more oily fish - or consuming omega-3's in other ways - promotes normal cardiovascular and immune function, and can help prevent or ease the symptoms of inflammatory and autoimmune disorders such as rheumatoid arthritis, Crohn's Disease, eczema, psoriasis and lupus, as well as certain forms of cancer. Omega-3 is also anti-thrombotic, lowers blood viscosity, promotes vasodilation, protects against arrythymias, promotes prostaglandin production and lowers blood pressure and triglycerides (blood fat levels).

However, the benefits to our mental health have been validated by research only relatively recently.

Basically, the omega-3's are essential for the optimal function of every cell in our bodies, especially our brains, where they are found in unusually high concentration (our brains are mostly water, but of the rest, some 60% is made up of polyunsaturated fatty acids). They are precursors to important signalling molecules and vital components of the healthy cell membrane, promoting efficient communication between neurones. We cannot manufacture them internally. Like vitamin C, calcium and many other crucial nutrients, the polyunsaturated fatty acids - including omega-3 and omega-6 - must be obtained via diet. How you might go about this will be discussed shortly and in the next chapter.

Before that, the evidence. Various findings point to a strong link between omega-3's and depression. I will mention a few of these.

First, there are interesting population studies linking the eating of large amounts of oily fish to lower rates of major depression. In industrialised countries such as the UK, where fish consumption has generally fallen in the last 100 years, the incidence of depression has risen. For example, those born before 1914 were about 100 times less likely to be depressed by the age of 45 than those born after 1945. Prior to industrialisation (that is, pre-1750s), omega-3's were more common elements of the human diet, derived largely from cold water oily fish, as well as wild animals and plants. And way back in the stone age, archaeologists argue that our common ancestor, homo habilis, evolved eating alot of omega-3 fatty acids. This was possibly essential to the evolution of our brains.

More striking is that, in the present-day, the rate of depression and heart disease in high fish-eating countries such as Japan, and among people such as the Inuit Indians in Alaska, is significantly lower than in countries such as the UK and USA, where more processed food and seed-oils (containing omega-6 fatty acids) are consumed. This is even when you consider the underreporting of psychiatric illness among the Inuits and Japanese. The rate of post-natal depression also seems to be lower in countries where fish is very popular. Mothers who regularly replenish their omega-3 reserves may be better protected against depressive symptoms (babies consume alot of omega-3 from the mother when breast-feeding).

All of this is not proof of causality of course, merely a strong series of correlations. There may be significant social factors which explain the differences between rates of depression among these socially different groups.

Second, people with clinical depression tend to have lower levels of omega-3 fatty acids in their blood. Omega-6 fatty acids tend to be more plentiful. As symptoms become more severe, the amount of omega-3 in the blood is likely to be lower still.

Again, a strong correlation, but not proof of a cause-and-effect relationship.

Third, the human brain does not seem to function optimally unless there are adequate amounts of omega-3 fatty acids circulating in the bloodstream and being incorporated into cell membranes. Animal studies have shown that the brain works better when omega-3 fatty acids are present to influence the brain chemicals involved in anti-depressant action (serotonin and noradrenaline).

Fourth, there have been studies by various researchers in the UK and USA that suggest the adding in of fish-oil capsules high in EPA (eicosapentanoic acid) can help people with depressive illness. DHA (docosahexaenoic acid) - another compound found in fish oil - appears important too, but not so much as EPA. For example, Stoll himself prescribed fish oil supplements to a small group of treatment-resistant depressive patients. The fish oil was in addition to their conventional anti-depressant. 22% of the group responded well, well above the 10% or so which might have been expected in a treatment-resistant population. Recently, in 2014, a comprehensive meta-analysis of randomised clinical trials (RCTs) was conducted by Giuseppe Grosso and his fellow researchers in America. RCTs are the gold standard in terms of proof required to back up scientific theories. From analysis of 19 separate trials they concluded that omega-3 EPA supplementation is effective in people with severe clinical depression. Hallahan and colleagues (2016) carried out a systematic review and meta-analysis of 35 double-blind RCTs from between 1980 and 2014. Their results also showed statistical significance for EPA-predominant omega-3 formulations in people with moderate-to-severe depression. On the other hand another review by Katharine Appleton and colleagues (2015) is less conclusive. And the SIGN and NICE Guidelines in the UK do not recommend their use in depression.

So overall, the jury is still out as regards definitive proof. **But in my mind the evidence is strong enough to act on now,** especially considering the safety, low financial cost and minimal side-effects involved in increasing your omega-3 intake. As part of taking more control and responsibility for your mental and physical health, you might want to give this a go.

Basic dietary advice will be covered in the next chapter. Information on omega-3 supplements is included here.

Omega-3 Supplements

Take good quality concentrated fish oil supplements high in EPA compared with DHA. The better quality a supplement, the less capsules you will need to take and the less chance of a fishy burp or "repeat". Also the better the refining process it will have been through, which filters out pollutants. A single dose usually come in the form of 1g or 1000g capsule, made up of EPA, DHA and other less useful fats. Total cumulative daily doses (EPA + DHA) of up to 3 grams, or 3000mg, are very safe. Optimum EPA dose varies ; Stoll recommends 1500-4000 mg per day, which in theory means swallowing up to 20 capsules every day! This of course is not feasible considering the cost, number of capsules and likelihood of fishy burps. However, in theory you could likely take even more if your stomach could tolerate it : the Inuit Indians of Alaska eat up to 19 grams of omega-3 a day, mostly in the form of whale and seal meat. They also have very low rates of heart disease and depression, although of course all of this may have more to do with their positive social support networks. Again, it is hard to prove one way or another.

Remember the available evidence points to EPA being more important in regulating mood. Affordable supplements can be bought from supermarkets, most good health stores and some pharmacists, but check the levels of EPA and DHA. Your doctor may also be willing to prescribe them for you (if your local NHS prescribing board allows it), but this is increasingly unlikely, especially in the UK. I used to have them prescribed adjunctively off-label by an open-minded GP, but this was stopped around 2012 and I have bought my own since.

The best quality fish oil supplement available is probably the one I used to take, a brand called Omacor, but it is quite expensive if you have to pay for it. It is commonly given to patients as a preventative treatment following a heart attack, because it has been proven to lower levels of triglycerides in the bloodstream. It has a high level of EPA in each capsule. The next best I have found in terms of EPA content is from the Holland & Barrett chain of health stores. But the NICE and SIGN Guidelines do not recommend omega-3 routinely as an adjunct for the treatment of depression : the evidence is there and accepted as promising, but it does not meet the high bar set by these bodies.

Interestingly, the respected psychiatrists' handbook, the Maudsley Prescribing Guidelines (2009), cautiously backs their use off-label as an adjunct to antidepressants in treatment-resistant depression and as an adjunct to antipsychotic medication in schizophrenia. This illustrates a willingness by the scientific and medical community to recommend more natural medications outwith the strict medical model. I would suggest that perhaps the potential large cost of making them available to people with depression (a far bigger group of people that those diagnosed with schizophrenia) plays a part in the lack of recommendation to date. Big pharma may also be at work in playing down the potential of a natural therapeutic agent, as there would not be much profit in it for them (no patents required, etc).

Importantly, if you are taking **warfarin or high doses of aspirin, please consult your doctor** if you are thinking about trying the fish oils. These and other related medications are blood-thinners ; taking fish-oils may lead to an over-thinning of the blood.

Lastly, **do not attempt to derive omega-3's from cod liver oil supplements** ; too much cod liver oil can be toxic due to the high levels of vitamin A involved.

Vegetarians can choose flaxseed oil supplements, walnuts or leafy green vegetables (eg purslane and broccoli) which are also high in omega-3 (albeit the shorter chain version, alpha-linolenic acid / ALA).

Supplements to augment the Omega-3s

Take a multi-vitamin supplement with a good dosage of the antioxidants, vitamin C and E. Or take separate supplements. The RDA is 60 mg/day for vitamin C and 15 IU/day for vitamin E. However, many nutritionists consider these RDA's to be inadequate and recommend upwards of 200mg/day (max 1000-2000mg) of vitamin C and 900 IU/day of vitamin E. These antioxidants neutralize the effects of toxic free radical molecules and help to boost the effectiveness of omega 3 in the cell membranes. So it follows that as taking omega-3s could help an antidepressant work better in the brain, taking vitamin C and E could enhance the effectiveness of both.

Interestingly, a recent large-scale study at John Hopkins University in Baltimore, USA, concluded that taking high doses of vitamins C and E led to people over 65 having a 70% lower risk of developing Alzheimers' Disease. So it looks like they have, at the very least, a general health-promoting effect on brain function.

Gingko Biloba may help improve blood circulation in the body, particularly to the brain. It is derived from a hardy tree that has grown for over 65 million years ; most likely the oldest tree species on earth. Ingesting the leaves has been strongly associated with improved memory function and many other positive physical benefits. So while gingko may not possess specific anti-depressant properties, it is harmless to take in recommended doses and may make a small but significant difference to blood flow to the depressed brain.

It is also worth noting that, not surprisingly, taking extra omega-3's is also advised for other mental illnesses. There is evidence to support their use in bipolar disorder, schizophrenia, post-natal depression and Attention Deficit Hyperactive Disorder (ADHD). Even people who are generally functioning well could improve their mental functioning with extra omega-3 fatty acids.

Before the next chapter, it is worth mentioning that if you have chosen to accept a prescription for orthodox antidepressants from your doctor, you may or may not be feeling a sense of shame or disappointment that you have "had to rely on pills". You might feel that you have "given in" to the depression in a way.

If you are thinking along those lines, try talking to yourself firmly but fairly. There does not have to be shame in taking antidepressants. You are suffering from a mental-physical illness which is proven to respond to antidepressant medication. If you were diabetic would you choose to go without insulin, if you were asthmatic would you refuse an inhaler, if you had parkinson's would you forego levodopa or other helpful medications ?

Of course, this is easy to say but often much harder to do. We can berate ourselves unfairly at times. But try not to feel any less a person if you have started them. You may only need to take them for 6 months (the usual minimum recommendation). Or like a diabetic or asthmatic, you may need maintenance medication over the long-term. In essence, rather than being a disaster or a capitulation, taking medication long-term or for a limited time can be a sensible and acceptable way of caring for yourself.

A mildish bout of depression may not require pharmacological help. On the other hand, surviving a severe episode without the support of medication is brave if you can do it. Some would say foolhardy. You could rationally choose not to take any, because bouts of depression have been shown to usually clear up of their own accord eventually. And some people have one major bout in their life and never need pills or treatment again. However, it can be a very long haul to get through a clinical episode of this illness. Think seriously about whether you want to tough it out on your own or accept a little bit of non-addictive pharmacological help.

It is your choice.

Chapter 4 : Diet

"You are what you eat" is an often-quoted old pearl of wisdom, arguably tainted by the controversial, questionably-qualified nutritionist Gillian McKeith in the early 2000's. My paternal grandmother was a staunch advocate of this approach. When I was in my teens and twenties I used to debate with her that noone could seriously take the view that diet accounts for everything. It is true to an extent, I would argue, particularly with regard to our physical health, but it is just one of loads of factors that contribute to our sense of mental health and wellbeing. In essence my belief has not changed, but if anything, I have moved a little in her direction. And if I am honest, in the course of the 13 years researching this book, and putting some dietary changes into practice, I have to say that I have edged further in her direction. Diet most certainly plays an important part in achieving good physical health ; and has been increasingly recognised as influential in achieving good mental health.

There is something very logical about following the chapter on medications with one on diet. Medication is, after all, strictly speaking, part of our diet. But it is most definitely a two-way street, as a good diet is also medicinal and health-promoting. There is certainly strong evidence in favour of some foods being therapeutic in depression.

Some might argue that, wait a minute, there are millions of people out there eating very poor diets, and not all of them are depressed. This would be true. A bad diet does not cause depression on its own. But this should not be used as an argument for continuing to eat unhealthy food. At least **your diet is a factor more within your control.** You can help yourself to feel better - or at least stop yourself from feeling worse - by taking on board some of the following advice.

Generally Speaking....

We all know (if someone doesn't, then they must have been hiding under a bush for the last 50 years) about the basics of a healthy diet. I refer to the established knowledge of the mainstream here, not to unorthodox diets such as Atkins, which are open to question as healthy options in the long-term. Figure 3 shows that pie chart illustration we have all seen somewhere, usually in a GP surgery.

Figure 3 : The Eatwell Chart

A diet which is high in fibre and carbohydrate, and low in fat, is generally accepted to be health-promoting.

High in fibre :

- Eating more fibre-rich, low sugar breakfast cereals (eg oatmeal porridge, bran flakes, muesli and all bran), and wholemeal, granary or seeded bread.
- Also eating fresh fruit and vegetables, ideally 5 portions a day in total. Dark green vegetables such as broccoli and spinach contain the most fibre.

More fibre promotes a healthy GI tract, with less risk of constipation and even bowel cancers. With recent research pointing to a staggering 1 in 2 UK citizens born after 1960 developing cancer at some point in their lives, this is a good enough reason in itself to instigate a thorough audit of what fuel we are putting into our bodies (whilst of course recognising that not all cancers are caused by poor diet in and of itself).

High in carbohydrate :

- Consuming more sources of slow-release energy eg wholemeal bread, pasta, rice and potatoes. One of the body's principal fuels, glucose, is largely derived from starch-rich foods such as these. Significantly, neurones (brain cells) rely heavily on glucose for their energy.
- Eating less processed / refined foods.

More carbohydrate helps to boost (or at least preserve) energy levels, and promotes sleep at night (providing they are not consumed too late in the evening).

Low in fat :

- Avoiding, as much as possible, foods which are high in saturated fats, trans-fatty acids and cholesterols. The more of these fats you eat, the heavier you are likely to become, and the greater your risk of heart disease, cancer, stroke and many other ailments . You won't be doing your mental health much good either. Depression is a tough enough illness to combat without the self-esteem sapping effects of putting on lots of weight. Even if eating these foods does not lead to weight gain, your energy levels are not optimised by a diet rich in such fats.
- Including more food in your diet which is high in monounsaturated and polyunsaturated acids, and omega-3 fatty acids (see later in chapter for more detailed discussion).

Other Tips

Those are the basics, most of which you probably knew anyway. However, you may be struggling with the age-old chestnut of it all being **easier said than done,** especially as we live in the UK, where foods rich in sugar and fat are cheap, convenient and readily available (the same goes for most westernised countries). Very few of us eat the perfect diet. It is likely to be even harder for you if you are depressed, because you may have limited energy for shopping. Even if you have the energy, you might be finding it really difficult to face people at the supermarket. And, even if you can push yourself to buy healthy food, what about the preparation and cooking of it all? Microwave, convenience foods and ready-to-eat stuff can seem very appealing, as well as comforting.

The healthy diet is an ideal to aspire to, not an absolute 100% must. It is not worth beating yourself up over the negatives in your diet. But it is worth thinking seriously about improving the quality of the fuel you put in your body, even just a little bit. This is particularly the case if you are depressed. A healthy diet can only help, it cannot harm. Here are a few more tips that could help :

- Drink more **water** and minimise sugary and fizzy drinks. Our bodies are over 80% water so this makes common sense. The majority of us don't drink enough, and this is associated with the onset of a whole host of ailments. The consensus recommendation is to drink somewhere between 1.5 and 2 litres a day. This helps to keep our urinary and GI tract flushed out, and our body and brain functioning optimally. Adequate intake of water also minimises 'snacking' or 'grazing', as very often we mistake thirst pangs for hunger pangs. Even if you can do nothing else, drinking a large glass of water first thing in the morning is at least a start. However, as with most things in life, "everything in moderation", as drinking too much water can lead to dilutional hyponatremia or "water intoxication".

- Monitor your **caffeine** intake. We are a nation of tea and coffee-drinkers and many of us overdo it. For a start, both are diuretics, meaning they make us run to the toilet more. Therefore they do not rehydrate us as well as regular water. And they are stimulants, putting us on edge if we drink a lot. I am not recommending you give up tea and coffee completely, as there are social and health benefits to drinking them in moderation, but it might be worth 1) getting into the habit of taking a drink of water before every cuppa, so as to rehydrate yourself properly, and 2) trying decaffeinated versions, or naturally caffeine-free herbal teas. For example, valerian tea, while smelling slightly suspect, can help with sleep and relaxation. So can passiflora and camomile. And peppermint and green tea help to aid digestion as well as provide a pleasant, refreshing caffeine-free alternative.

- Avoid excessive **alcohol**, especially when depressed. It is a CNS (Central Nervous System) depressant. If you want to drink when you are well, be sensible about your intake. Overdoing it only increases the risk of relapse. Be mindful of context, that is who you are drinking with – you might be fine having a couple of drinks with a close friend, but you might be putting yourself at enormous risk drinking with larger groups of friends and acquaintances who may not necessarily be holding your best interests as a priority. Take responsibility for yourself and your welfare. Look at it another way. Imagine a good friend of yours was a diagnosed diabetic who gave into temptation one day. A binge on chocolate and sweets ensued. Their blood sugar levels became hyperglycaemic and they developed acute ketoacidosis, requiring intravenous infusion of saline and emergency insulin. You would likely empathise with them - I mean they're only human like you after all - but you would also be justified in pointing out that they played a role in their own downfall.

- Eat nuts, (preferably unsalted, so as to keep blood pressure down) wholegrains, avacado, brown rice, and oatmeal. These are examples of good sources of **vitamin E** - a potent antioxidant - which can help prevent the formation of damaging free-radical molecules and defend healthy cell membranes against free-radical attack. This has the added benefit of aiding the metabolism of omega-3 fatty acids and selenium inside the cell membrane. If you feel unsure of your ability to get enough vitamin E in your diet, you can opt for a supplement of up to about 900 iu per day.

- Increase your intake of **selenium**, another effective antioxidant which possesses even greater potency if you are getting plenty of vitamin E in your diet. Natural sources include garlic, onions, fish, shellfish, red grapes, broccoli, whole wheat, eggs and chicken. In supplement form, 50-100 mcg is enough. (Regarding garlic specifically, remember it has other therapeutic properties such as being antibiotic, antifungal, anticancerous and procardiovascular. You may want to consider an odour-free supplement).

- Make sure you are getting enough **vitamin C** for the same reasons as above, as it is also an antioxidant. In addition, the human body requires vitamin C to form collagen, the substance which binds together the cells of connective tissue. Hence, if a person suffers from scurvy, caused by a lack of vitamin C, they tend to bleed alot, internally and externally. Vitamin C is also essential for an effective immune system, helping to prevent viruses from entering the cell membrane. Good food sources include oranges, apples, strawberries, kiwi fruit, blueberries, grapefruit, red peppers, brussel sprouts, melons, mango, cranberry juice, potatoes with skin, and tomatoes. If you find it difficult to consume enough vitamin C in your diet, choose a supplement of up to 1000-2000mg per day. Unlike the insoluble vitamins A and D, the body will excrete the water soluble vitamin C it does not require, but this is no reason to overdose on it. Interestingly, vitamin C combined with 15 mg a day of zinc appears to be very effective in combatting and preventing the common cold.

- Cook with extra virgin olive oil or canola oil. These contain the least amount of saturated fat.

- If possible, **grill or bake** your food rather than fry.

- **Spread butter or margarine thinly** on bread.

- **Try to take tea and coffee without sugar.** Weaning yourself off gradually is more likely to lead to success.

- Generally eat less foods that are high in **sugar.**

I have separated off the next 2 sub-sections because they are potentially very important and deserve to be given little blurbs of their own : probiotics and omega-3's in the diet.

Probiotics

- Eat more turkey, chicken, bananas, eggs, nuts, wheat germ, avacodos, milk, cottage cheese, cheese, peas, beans, onions, garlic, chilli, oats, barley, chickpeas and lentils. These are foods sometimes referred to as **prebiotics**, naturally rich in tryptophan, an amino acid and precursor of serotonin in the brain. Smaller amounts are found in wholemeal breads, cereals, potatoes and rice. Many of these foods are also high in fibre. You will recall that serotonin is one of the important mood-regulating neurotransmitters found in the brain. Therefore, by eating these foods consistently as part of a normal healthy diet, we can naturally and subtly boost our mood.

- Eat more **probiotic / fermented** food and drinks. For example, miso soup (no more than 1 a day due to high salt content), ginger beer, sourdough bread, sauerkraut, kombucha tea, kimchi, kefir and natural probiotic yoghurts (natural yoghurt is healthier than fruit-flavoured), to promote balance between the "good" and "bad" bacteria in your gut. These foods contain probiotic bacteria such as lactobacillus acidophilus, lactobacillus helveticus, bifidobacterium longum and bifidobacterium bifidum. In recent years such foods have been termed **psychobiotics** by some. This is because there is increasing evidence that our GI tract has a big influence on our mood. In fact as much as 90% of our serotonin and other neurotransmitters may be produced here, a process enhanced by a healthy intake of the amino-acid tryptophan, prebiotics and probiotics.

- A healthy balance of gut bacteria also looks like it promotes a more positive response to stress and lowered inflammation levels (which is related to good mental health). There is scientific evidence to back such claims up and a recent systematic review and meta-analysis of available randomised controlled studies in August 2016 (Nutrients 8(8), 483) strongly supported the use of probiotics in depression. But large-scale studies remain to be published. However, rather than waiting around for definitive proof, it would appear eminently sensible to give some of these options a go in moderation. Like the omega-3's, there is good evidence that they are not harmful in moderate doses, they are beneficial to your physical health, and in all likelihood they are positive for your psychological health.

- There is a useful analogy between tending to a garden and looking after your gut. The "fertiliser" is provided by regular consumption of prebiotic and tryptophan-containing foods. This fosters an environment that helps to promote the growth of the "good" bacteria, provided by probiotic foods. That is, the "good" bacteria has plenty to feed off. Avoiding too much sugar helps to keep the "weeds" ("bad" bacteria) to a minimum. Keeping well hydrated helps to water the "garden". And last but not least, be patient, as it takes a while for the garden to grow and become established.

If you can manage all of the above you will be doing amazingly well. If you can manage even half of it you'll still be doing great (I am probably doing about 60-70% ; I still eat too much sugar in the form of chocolate and biscuits). And even a few changes is better than nothing.

Omega-3's in the Diet

Following on from the discussion of omega-3 supplements in the previous chapter, here is some sensible advice as regards increasing your intake in your everyday diet. Dieticians have been recommending omega-3's for a long, long time, because the evidence for benefit to physical health is so strong and unambiguous. So the advice is to eat more of them anyway. In reality for the depressed person, it is something of a bonus that the omega-3 fatty acids also appear to possess mood-enhancing properties.

There is a little repetition of chapter 3 here. As was mentioned in the introduction, this is probably not a bad thing considering your fragile concentration :

- Eat more oily fish (eg salmon, mackerel, herring, sardines, pilchards, anchovies, kippers, halibut). These species eat a lot of omega-3 rich marine plant life called phytoplankton. They are higher in omega-3 fatty acids compared with white fish, because it is stored in their flesh (muscles) rather than their livers (which is the case for white fish such as cod and haddock). Two portions of fish per week is recommended by the World Health Organisation (WHO), including one portion of oily fish. The benefits are physical as well as psychological. For example, as mentioned in ch.3, the omega-3s protect against heart disease by lowering blood pressure, blood cholesterol and triglyceride (blood fat) levels. They promote arterial elasticity and vasodilation, and protect against arrythmia (irregular heartbeat). They are also natural blood thinners, thereby protecting against blood clots that can lead to heart attack or stroke. Furthermore, they are anticancerous and antiinflammatory, being particularly useful in psoriasis, arthritis, crohn's disease, asthma and lupus.

Recent evidence shows that the level of omega-3s in farmed salmon has halved since 2011, compared with wild atlantic salmon (bbc.co.uk, 6th October 2016). This is to do with the decreasing amounts of omega-3 in the farmed fish' diet (to do with environmental concerns about over-use of anchovies), compared with the wild salmon diet rich in krill and anchovies. As many of us buy our salmon from supermarkets it is likely that we are unwittingly consuming less omega-3's than we may think. So researchers at Stirling University are now recommending that the eaters of farmed salmon consume 2 of these oily fish portions per week, along with 1 non-oily.

- Tuna is a less reliable source of omega-3. It depends on the species, with albacore tuna the best. Environmental pollution may be more of a problem compared with other fish species. One regular-sized can is the accepted safe limit per week.

- Vegetarians can combine flaxseeds or flaxseed oil supplements with dark green leafy vegetables, walnuts and purslane. These are all rich in the shorter chain omega-3, alpha-linolenic acid (ALA).

- Wild game meat (such as venison, buffalo, bison and pheasant) is an option if you can source it, if you like it and if you can afford it, as it contains x7 more shorter-chain omega-3 than commercial meat. The reason being the animals have run around in the wild and eaten a more varied, natural diet, so are leaner as a result.

- Remember that nutritionists recommend that we aim for a diet that contains about the same amount of omega-6 compared with omega-3. This is based on the diet our common ancestors ate, the diet which is most suited to our biology. As a species we have evolved over millions of years, yet our diets have only become omega-6 dominated in the last 300. We are not designed to be eating so much grain, saturated fat, and sugar. Current estimates are that we consume, on average, 10-20 times more omega-6 than omega-3. There is obviously vast room for improvement.

In summary, remember the basics of a healthy diet. Try to incorporate the principles of rehydration, low fat, high carbohydrate and high fibre into your daily eating habits. Be aware of the mood-enhancing prebiotic foods like bananas containing tryptophan, the precursor to serotonin. Increase your intake of probiotic foods like natural yoghurt and miso soup containing "good" bacteria. If you think you are not getting enough nutrition from your diet, consider taking vitamin C, vitamin E, selenium and garlic supplements for their health-promoting antioxidant properties. On top of this, try to increase your intake of omega-3 fatty acids, either via your diet, supplements, or ideally both. Even a small change in your diet could make a difference to your mood.

Top-Down

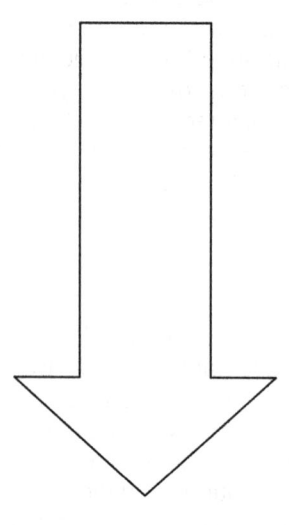

Chapter 5 : Thoughts

"Happiness doesn't depend on outward conditions, it depends on inner conditions. It isn't what you have or who you are or what you are doing that makes you happy or unhappy. It is what you think about."

Dale Carnegie (author of "How to Win Friends and Influence People", c.1945)

"Men are disturbed not by things, but by the views which they take of them"

Epictetus, c.107 AD

You might think that a chapter on thoughts in a book about depression would be quite lengthy. On the contrary I have chosen to keep this relatively short, because I believe that the key message for you to take away is that **our thoughts in depression are to be treated with a big pinch of salt.** They are, on the whole, not to be trusted. As a patient at work said recently to me : "depression is a liar".

It is in the aftermath of a depressive episode that most cognitive (thinking) progress can be made. Furthermore I believe that during a depressive episode it is how we choose to behave that is of more importance (see chapter 6). However, there are still helpful ways of approaching our thoughts within depression that are worth discussing.

It has been estimated that somewhere between 30,000 and 50,000 thoughts enter our minds every single day. These thoughts comprise a huge variety, ranging from the uplifting, inspirational, positive and helpful, to the mundane and neutral, all the way through to the worrying, self-deprecating, potentially disturbing, downright bizarre, negative and unhelpful. Even the most optimistic and well-balanced of individuals will encounter such unhelpful thoughts, albeit less in terms of quantity and severity.

Most thoughts appear in our minds uninvited, like gate-crashers at a party. Some are pleasant, benign, neutral and harmless, while some have the potential to do us damage if we blindly accept them or over-react to them. If you are already low in self-esteem, these negative thoughts can feel stronger, more threatening and more intense (that is, you will likely feel like giving in to them or over-reacting to them). You can potentially perceive them as more scary than they really are, like the long shadow of a small person on a wall (if you have ever read the book or watched the TV adaptation of the popular childrens' story "The Gruffalo", you will appreciate what I am saying here). The key word here is potentially. **Our thoughts do not have to define us.** We have choices. We can learn to deal with our negative, unhelpful thoughts more constructively. We can take a step back from them, see them from a distance and see them for what they really are.

Of note, practitioners of meditation and mindfulness often think of thoughts as being like autumn leaves floating down a river. They see themselves as impartial observers of these leaves, from the perspective of sitting on the river bank. From this detached position they remind themselves that they are in a position to choose which thoughts (leaves) to examine, and which they are going to simply allow to float on by.

This is a most helpful metaphor if you are generally coping ok with life. However, if you are struggling for whatever reason, it can be extremely difficult to leave the "leaves", or negative thoughts, alone. In essence it can feel like there is a hurricane at our back and the riverbank is wet and slippery, putting us in danger of falling into the river, to be swamped by our thoughts. The negative thoughts can persist and fight for our attention, like those annoying gate-crashers incessantly ringing the doorbell, or debris caught in a swirling river eddy. This can tire us and leave us vulnerable to them. It is **difficult but not impossible** to deal with them. We can essentially dismiss them, or if we think it is worth it, we can deal with them assertively. The right medication (chapter 3), dietary (chapter 4) and behaviour choices (chapter 6) can also combine to help us enormously.

Let us return to that distinction between dealing with unhelpful thoughts during and after a depressed episode.

During a Depressed Episode

When you're in the midst of a depressive episode your negative thoughts and imagery dominate. They appear in your mind without invitation and they come at you so thick and fast, they hardly give you a break. It is a bit like being caught in a blizzard or torrential storm. All you can really do is psychologically pitch your tent, batton down the hatches, keep yourself occupied with non-threatening activity (more on this in chapter 6) and eventually see out the storm. When the storm lifts (as storms always do), you can inspect the damage and go about making repairs, strengthening your tent pegs and tent structure in a bid to improve your ability to cope with whatever life throws at you going forward. If a particularly "violent" storm / depressive episode hits you, you might discover that you've pitched your tent on quicksand. You might feel that you are starting to sink. The temptation is to start panicking, to fight and struggle, but this is a mistake. You need to keep your head (quite a challenge when others around you may be losing theirs). If you know anything about quicksand, the last thing you want to do is struggle and squirm, as you will inevitably sink quicker. It is best to stay as calm as possible (this is **difficult, not impossible**), try to distract yourself with non-threatening activity, wait for the "rain to stop", and accept help (in no particular order).

Even strong and robust people can get clinically depressed. Most of us have our breaking point. If an otherwise balanced and healthy person is unlucky enough to be hit by a series of big stressful events (eg a really unlucky sequence of significant bereavement, divorce, illness and job loss), there is the chance that he/she will be "tipped over the edge" into clinical depression. There's a song from 1944 that my dad used to love, by the old-fashioned Rhythm and Blues group, The Ink Spots, along with Ella Fitzgerald. They sing soulfully that "Into each life some rain must fall, but too much has fallen in mine." So most of us can be overwhelmed by stress and very few of us are immune to depression.

It really is quite striking how negative your thinking can be in clinical depression. There is no other species who can turn on itself so viciously. As I have learned about the illness down the years, I have become more able to distance myself from these thoughts when suffering from a bout. That is not to say I have overcome them there and then, as I have still felt to varying extents mentally and physically imprisoned in my mind and body. But I have managed to regularly remind myself that these thoughts do not define me. Most of them are just **opinions, not facts.** Just because I am thinking them, does not make them real or true.

As my overall awareness of the illness has grown, so has my **ability to notice the negative thoughts**. This is crucial so as to avoid them sneaking in unexamined, "under the radar", potentially doing ourselves damage. This can sometimes be quite difficult, what with all of the other things we have to attend to in life. But we can learn to be more alert to these rogue thoughts. Once spotted, we can label them as unhelpful, challenge them or dismiss them, then proceed to get back to what we were doing. Or if we were sitting and ruminating at the time of the thought, we can start to do something distracting (see chapter 6 for more distraction strategies).

In the beginning I would get myself tied up in knots trying to argue against my thoughts, or somehow in vain try to push them out of my head. Witness my first spell of illness when I was 20 - 21 (see chapter 1) of fruitlessly researching the evidence for the existence of both god and evolution. I have never gone down that dead-end route again because I soon appreciated that **"...this is clinical depression, a mental and physical illness. Many of my thoughts are unhelpful and misleading. Life may feel meaningless and pointless at the moment, but this will pass and I will feel better again"**.

Note : my personal experience of the illness is such that I cannot deal with my depressive thoughts on my own. I also need preventative medication, a decent diet, good social support, structure to my days and constructive activity. I also do best when avoiding alcohol. You may be similar to me, or you may be able to deal with your thoughts constructively without recourse to some or all of these options.

After a Depressed Episode

Like any other illness, once better, your goal is to stay better and try to reduce the chances of relapse. Cognitive-Behavioural Therapy

(CBT) strategies can help enormously. You may have heard of CBT, it is the most available of the psychological therapies in the UK and has a huge evidence base behind it. We will start with the C in CBT. It stands for Cognitive, which is Latin for thinking. Once you have survived a bout of clinical depression, once you have emerged out the other side (which can happen anytime, sometimes when you least expect it, and sometimes just after things have seemed at their darkest) you can really benefit from reading about or engaging in CBT. This can be via telephone support, e-learning (eg www.livinglifetothefull.com or www.beatingtheblues.co.uk, www.getselfhelp.co.uk, and www.moodgym.anu.edu.au, www.cci.health.wa.gov.au), community talks, small groups, or individual CBT with a psychologist or psychological therapist (the latter can usually be accessed through your GP, through the NHS, or with a private provider).

The first goal in Cognitive Therapy is to increase awareness of our **thinking errors.** These are common mistakes we all occasionally make with our automatic thinking. People with low self-esteem make these mistakes more frequently. Put simply, we latch on to threatening and negative thoughts we would otherwise not bother with, or easily dismiss. People with clinical depression (which is often mixed with anxiety) are prone to believe all of their thinking errors. Take a look at the following list and ask yourself if you have been habitually making these errors of late :

- **Catastrophising, involving "grasshopper thinking".** That is, jumping to the worst conclusions by making huge, irrational leaps in logic. For example, if you perceive that your short-term memory has been failing you of late you may jump to the conclusion that your brain is permanently damaged. Or if someone doesn't see you in the street you may conclude that they obviously despise me, like everyone does, because I am unloveable

- **Predicting the worst.** "Gloomy fortune-telling". Similar to catastrophising.

- **Mind-reading.** Based on minimal evidence, jumping to conclusions regarding what others are thinking (eg believing that others think ill of you, that others think you think ill of them, that others judge you negatively and / or don't like you).

- **Taking on too much responsibility.** Taking things to heart or unfairly taking the blame for something. Sometimes we can be partly responsible for something but unfortunately and mistakenly blame ourselves 100%.

- **All-or-Nothing thinking.** Extreme "black-and-white" thinking eg seeing people as saints or sinners, good or bad, with little room for grey areas. Or situations as great or awful, with no acknowledgement of simply "ok" or "good enough" in the middle.

- **Over-generalising.** For example, just because you haven't done well in something, it doesn't mean you are rubbish at everything.

- **Filtering out the positive.** Focussing on the negative in situations, looking through dark tinted glasses.

- **Emotional Reasoning.** Letting your emotions overly-guide your thinking.

- **Making extreme statements / rules** – excessive use of the words *always, never, must, should , ought or got to.*

Once we are aware of the common thinking errors we are making, we can go about challenging them via the use of **thought records.** Christine Padesky and Dennis Greenberger are probably the most famous exponents of the thought record, borne out of the work of Aaron T Beck, the father of cognitive therapy. They wrote an extremely readable CBT self-help book in 1995 called "Mind over Mood", which has been used extensively throughout the world (latest estimate of copies sold stands at over 1 million). A second edition has recently been published. In it they gradually introduce the concept of the thought record, using case examples and exercises for the reader to try. I thoroughly recommend this book if you want to read more than my brief overview of CBT.

I was introduced to the thought record back in 2006 when I worked on my own thinking errors for about 6 sessions with a very good CBT Therapist in Ayrshire. I got in to the habit of filling one out whenever I noticed a significant drop in my mood. I still fill them out occasionally to this day, and I encourage most of my patients to do the same. With practice and experience most people develop the ability to fill them out mentally in their heads.

Below is a seven column thought record (figure 4) (see www.getselfhelp.co.uk or "Mind over Mood" for printable copies).

You will see that column 1 is for noting the date, time and situation in which you noticed your mood change. Complete this in some detail, as it can help aid recall when you look back over your thought records in the future. Column 2 is for recording the emotion/s you felt at the time, and assigning a subjective percentage to those emotions (for example, 100% anxiety would be the most you have ever experienced, while 50% anxiety would be about half the intensity of that). Column 3 is for writing down the negative automatic thoughts you noticed **just before** you started to feel negative. The idea here is that you write as many of these down as you can recall, then assess which one of them was the "hottest", or potentially most distressing. Then you simply circle this "hot thought" and proceed to column 4, where you think of evidence to support it (this may seem odd, but I will explain in one of the following paragraphs). In column 5 you think of evidence against your chosen hot thought, then in column 6 you combine columns 4 + 5 and generate a balanced, alternative, "synthesised" thought. Column 7 simply involves a re-evaluation of your emotions, hopefully leading to an improvement in your mood. You may not feel this immediately, but often a person's mood may improve a few hours later. Most people will say that the more often they complete thought records, the greater the positive effect on their mood.

Figure 4 : Example of a Thought Record

Situation	Emotions	Automatic Thoughts	Evidence For the Hot Thought	Evidence Against the Hot Thought	Balanced Alternative Thought	Re-rate Emotions
A friend walked by me in the street and did not acknowledge me. Saturday 22/2 @ 3pm	Anxiety 80% Sadness 60% Anger 40%	I must have done something to them. They must not like me. **Everyone hates me.**	She seemed to ignore me. People often do that when they don't like someone. Maybe my other friends also quietly despise me.	I got on with her fine last week. She seemed preoccupied. I know she has her troubles too. A one-off incident like that does not mean that everyone hates me.	I think she was probably caught up in her own thinking. I will give her a phone to check how she is. My friends and family might occasionally get frustrated with me but I have plenty of evidence they have time for me.	Anxiety 50% Sadness 50% Anger 20%

96

Some may ask why pick out one "hot thought" when it is usually a whole batch of negative thoughts appearing together that challenges our mental equilibrium. The answer to this is simply that it is more manageable to focus on one. If we tried to challenge all of our negative automatic thoughts during or after a given significant situation it would take a heck of a long time and make for a very complex and labour-intensive thought record. By taking one thought designated as the "hottest", we learn the process of objectively challenging our thoughts without feeling overwhelmed.

The process of thinking of evidence to "support" your unhelpful negative thought sounds counter-intuitive in many ways. People often say that they "should be thinking more positively", so how can you do that when you are trying to think of evidence to back up some extremely negative thought ? The answer is that we can only think more helpfully and positively by thinking in a more balanced way. This is exactly why I discussed suicide statistics in chapter 1. The "old school" approach was to avoid discussion of such things, for fear of "giving people ideas". Well that is plainly wrong in the case of discussing suicide, and it is plainly wrong when it comes to weighing up your negative thoughts. The evidence shows that it is helpful to discuss the negative, because it may be partly true, and therefore helps us arrive at more balanced conclusions. If you simply try to push a negative thought out of your head, it will muscle its way back in again. Alternatively, if you treat it calmly and respectfully and weigh it up against other evidence, you have a much better chance of managing the thought (and ultimately your mood) to your own benefit. .

I like to think of the thought record as a tool to help you get the "chaos out of your head" and on to paper in a structured manner, where your healthy self is taking control, rather than feeling completely lost and at mercy to the thoughts of the depressed self. Some people say to me that they keep a diary, so that should be good enough. I question this, because as a keeper of a diary on-and-off myself for many years up until my early 30's, I know how unstructured, meandering, lamenting and ultimately unhelpful journal diaries can be. Quite simply, in my opinion, the thought record is the single most helpful and constructive cognitive tool ever developed.

From another perspective, novel neurobiological pathways are laid down the more one thinks in the manner of a thought record. Your brain heals and develops adaptively as you change your thinking habits. By way of another metaphor, imagine someone walks their dog along the same path, around the same field, for years and years on end. Eventually he/she decides that they have had enough of this route, they have got into a bit of a rut, and they opt for a change. They start to walk a different route on previously untrampled grass. Of course it takes a while for the new path to be flattened out and feel familiar. The old path remains tempting to use, indeed the dogwalker occasionally uses it on autopilot when they are thinking of other things. But over time, with conscious effort to start with, then habitually, this person regularly chooses the new path more often than the old path. The new path becomes established and the old path becomes overgrown and rarely used. So it is with our thinking – old habits can be changed.

If you want to learn more about CBT once you feel better, "Mind over Mood" is a good start. In fact it may be all you require. At this juncture I do not believe there is much to be gained in the context of this book by going into more detail. There is obviously a lot more to CBT, which I will try to summarise.

If you dig deeper past your negative automatic thoughts you will find **underlying assumptions and core beliefs** influencing how we think about ourselves, others and the world around us. **Core beliefs** are often learned early in life in order to fit into our family system, but they can develop in adulthood too, especially after a traumatic event like a car-crash or assault, when our beliefs about the safety of the world can be shattered. They can be learned directly and indirectly, from parents, siblings, influential adult-figures, school and culture / society. Inference and interpretation of events can play a big role (see the Epictetus quote at the beginning of the chapter).

Imagine a child being told constantly by a parent that they are stupid and a waste of space. A robust child might fight against this, raising a symbolic V sign against the message, and go on to spend their entire life proving their parent wrong. Perhaps working themselves into an early grave. However a vulnerable, less confident child could interpret this as meaning "They are right, I am stupid and not as important as others", leading to a tendency to put themselves down and underachieve in adulthood. Related negative automatic thoughts might arise frequently, such as "that person is better than me, I am stupid, I always have been", or "I got a good result there but I must have been lucky, or someone else must have performed badly for me to do well".

Another hypothetical child in a large family may jump to the wrong conclusion about something and form an unhelpful core belief to carry into adulthood. For example, the child who is often sent away to auntie's house for the weekend while her siblings spend more time with mum and dad. This child may carry bitterness and rejection into adulthood when in actual fact her parents simply sent her to aunt's house because aunt yearned for children and did not have any, and they decided to let her see a lot of their most easy going child. The big issue here is what has gone unsaid.

No matter what our underlying negative core beliefs and assumptions about the world, the challenge for all of us is to become more aware of what these are, and to work around them as much as possible. This is **difficult, not impossible.**

Stress-vulnerability model

Here we look briefly at the bigger picture. The stress-vulnerability model (figure 5, over the page) is well worth a mention as it emphasises what was said earlier in the chapter, that pretty much anyone can develop a mental health problem if put under enough stress. It goes against the idea that there are mentally ill people and mentally healthy people ; the "them and us" mentality. The more stress you perceive, the more likely you are to "cross over" into clinical depression and/or anxiety. Someone with high vulnerability to the effects of stress (who is further to the right hand side of the 'vulnerability' line in the graph below) will cross over into the 'mental health problem' area at lower amounts of stress (lower down the 'stress' line on the graph). Similarly someone with low vulnerability will cross over the line only when they experience higher amounts of stress.

Basically someone above the red line will not be coping very well, someone below the red line will be coping ok.

Figure 5 : The Stress Vulnerability Model

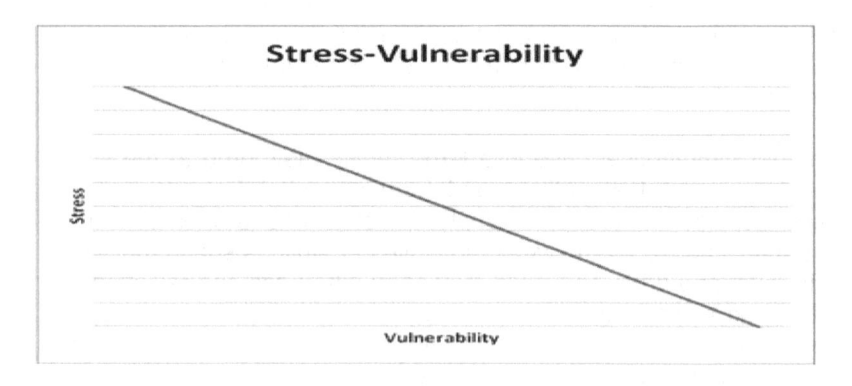

Stress-Vulnerability

[graph showing a downward sloping line, Y-axis labelled "Stress", X-axis labelled "Vulnerability"]

Just where each person's limit is set is determined by a number of factors. Genetics has a role, but so does our personal history and our ability to deal with issues and learn from our experiences. Similarly, what counts as stress can differ from person to person: one person's overwhelming problem could be another's exciting challenge. The meaning of the source of the stress is important and how it is interpreted can again depend on a number of factors, including personal history and ability to solve problems.

It can be tempting to think "if I can just minimise stress in my life I can minimise my chances of getting depressed or anxious". This is helpful but it is also important to recognise that a moderate amount of stress is accepted as a good thing; it makes us more alert and engaged with life. Just as too much stress can cause burn-out, so not enough can lead to what some occupational psychologists call 'rust-out' (see figure 6 overleaf). It is "everything in moderation" again.

Figure 6 : Model of Performance vs Anxiety

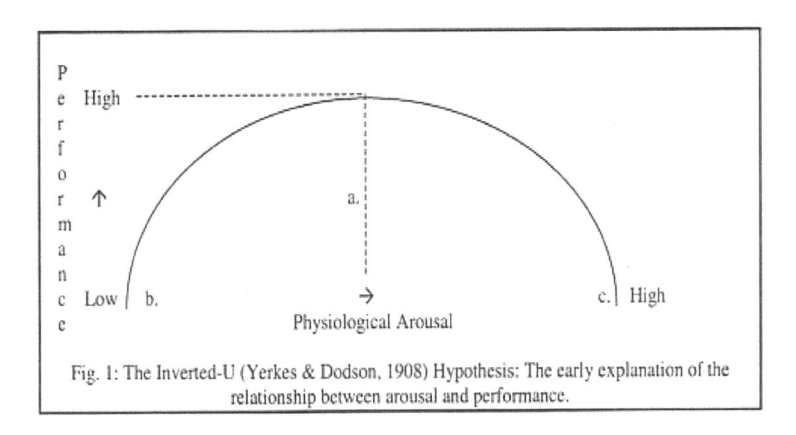

```
P
e  High ----------------------
r                    /    |    \
f                   /     |     \
o                  /      |      \
r   ↑             /       a.      \
m                /        |        \
a               /         |         \
n              /          |          \
c  Low  b.              →              c.  High
e                 Physiological Arousal
```

Fig. 1: The Inverted-U (Yerkes & Dodson, 1908) Hypothesis: The early explanation of the relationship between arousal and performance.

The amount of stress we experience also varies - we all have periods that are more stressful than others. Sometimes we can predict and prepare for stress, and sometimes it comes out of the blue. Similarly, our vulnerability to stress may vary over time - youth may make us more resilient in some ways, but age and experience can also help us keep a calm head where previously we may have fretted.

This makes the stress-vulnerability model a flexible way of looking at your work-life balance, helping you to avoid becoming overwhelmed and depressed. It cannot guarantee staying well, but it can promote wellness. It also serves to highlight that we benefit from taking a reasonable amount of responsibility for our own health, by choosing ways of living that minimise stress [for example, being consistently assertive (see more in chapter 6), avoiding excessive alcohol and drugs, keeping fit, eating a healthy diet, taking prescribed medications that are helpful, and so on].

I think my maternal grandmother summed stress up pretty well. Upon hearing of other peoples' struggles she would often remark ".....whose load would you lift ?" She had a good understanding of stress and struggle being universal. It is very much in our interest to accept that stress is inevitable at times, but we also do well to recognise that we have some control over how much it affects us. In the context of what we have discussed in this chapter, thought records are potentially a very useful tool in this regard.

Chapter 6 : Behaviour

"Don't wait to feel better before you start to do things, start doing things in order to feel better".

Anon

"Live life according to a plan, not a mood"

Anon

When in the midst of clinical depression, a person benefits from keeping themselves "ticking over" as much as they can. Related mantras I use very often with myself, and suggest to others, are : **don't wait to feel better before you start to do things, start doing things in order to feel better ; live life according to a plan not a mood** and **to feel valuable, act like you have value.** This type of approach is massively important. I believe this 100%. I would go as far to say that I believe the B in CBT to be slightly more important than the C.

As covered in chapter 5 our thoughts can be noticed and challenged assertively to our advantage, but changing our behaviour can do more. Doing so can achieve noticeable results around us **as well as** have a positive effect on our thinking. Pushing yourself to paint a bedroom wall, or weed part of the garden, or declutter a cupboard, may not help you feel much better as you do it, but you will at least fill your time constructively, and you will feel pleased with yourself once you start to recover. If there is a critical voice badgering you, saying that "you're not doing it right", "you've missed a bit", that "you are a useless piece of sh*t", or whatever....... accept that it's there, but take it with a pinch of salt and don't act on it, it will fade as you recover.

Of course, engaging in activity when you are depressed is far from easy, it requires a huge effort. You might just be aiming to dry a few dishes after tea, whilst the bulk of you wants to retreat to your bedroom and curl up under the duvet. Again, remind yourself that this is **difficult, not impossible.** Note that the CBT model (figure 7) illustrates the potential knock-on effects of making positive changes to your thoughts and behaviour. Both have a direct influence on your emotions and physiology. It is a very user-friendly and hopeful model, in that any positive change made in any area can contribute to reversing the **vicious cycle of depression**. For example, engage in Progressive Muscle Relaxation and Slow Breathing exercises, together with noticing and challenging negative thinking, accepting your emotions for what they are, and gradually overcoming your avoidant behaviour, and you are likely to eventually be rewarded with a more **virtuous cycle of recovery**.

Figure 7 : The CBT Model

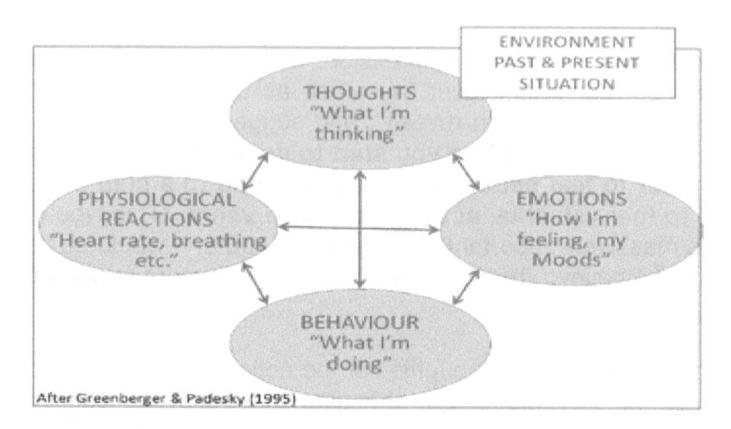

```
ENVIRONMENT
PAST & PRESENT
SITUATION

THOUGHTS
"What I'm thinking"

PHYSIOLOGICAL REACTIONS
"Heart rate, breathing etc."

EMOTIONS
"How I'm feeling, my Moods"

BEHAVIOUR
"What I'm doing"
```
After Greenberger & Padesky (1995)

Helpful Activity

When I suggest "ticking over" and "doing stuff" when you're depressed, it would help to be more specific. What I am really talking about is doing **"non-threatening activity."** (remember this terminology was first mentioned in the introduction). What this turns out to be very much depends on you. Basically, whatever you judge to be relatively non-threatening, is valid.

Let's first look at the basics, which I believe are your first priority. There are certain behaviours all of us can benefit from if we are depressed. Even if you wake up at half four in the morning full of dread, and just want to stay there and hide away from the world, try to push yourself to get out of bed at a consistent, reasonable time every day eg between 0700 and 0900 (you can push that back a bit at weekends if you like eg 0800 - 1000). If you usually shower every day, then keep showering every day, even if it feels really tough to do so. If you normally shower very two days, stick to that. Brush your teeth, dress yourself reasonably, present yourself as well as you usually would, but be mindful of context : if you are at home then I would suggest no need for excessive grooming or make-up, just stick to being reasonably clean and well-kempt. Do your laundry as regularly as you do when you are well. Fuel yourself with a healthy breakfast (keep chapter 4 in mind) and ensure that you eat lunch and dinner. **Treat yourself like you have value, even if you loathe yourself.**

The only exception to pushing yourself to get up at a regular time might be the first full day you experience depressed symptoms. I think it is usually the case that you are physically exhausted at this point. I tend to allow myself a few extra hours in bed that first day, to help cope with this exhaustion. Providing I can sleep that is – if I cannot get over to sleep I get up. From day 2 though, I am strict with myself about getting up and keeping occupied.

As for non-threatening activities to occupy the rest of the day, here are some that I find minimally threatening, in no particular order. The general rule is to stick to the familiar. Stick to activities you already know about or are simple to do, because your concentration is poor. Keep new learning and planning ahead to a minimum.

- Hoover, clean, mop, dust, iron, change the bedding, sort out the recycling, take the bins out.
- Do the dishes, load / empty the dishwasher, keep the kitchen clean and tidy.
- Load the washing machine and hang the clothes out to dry.
- Prepare and eat simple, healthy meals, and try to minimise snacking or comfort-eating.
- Get out for a long walk (or a jog if you feel up for it). If you have a dog you are well placed. (Our old family dog was at its fittest when I was ill ☺. I would walk her slowly for 5-6 miles on the local beach). But even if it's a short walk, at least you are putting one foot in front of the other. That's got to be better than sitting and dwelling.

- Any other form of exercise you think you can handle. It's about you taking control, acting in an anti-depressant way.
- Non-complicated do-it-yourself painting at a sensible, achievable pace (eg emulsion slowly onto walls ; but probably not gloss onto intricate skirting boards).
- Simple gardening, "keep nature at bay" (eg weeding, cutting grass,raking, trimming bushes, edging, painting a fence, wire-brushing the weeds in the gaps between patio stones). If you don't have a garden, get some house-plants and / or window boxes and look after them. In the early days of my depression an uncle of mine who I respect said to me that when he feels down, he gardens. I took this on board and it has helped me at times.
- Wipe down external window sills and window frames. Both inside and out, it is probably best to avoid climbing up ladders due to your struggle to concentrate.
- Tidy and de-clutter a room in the house, or the garage, or the shed, or even just one drawer. Do so at a manageable, achievable pace. It might be worth asking the opinion of others on this, as you may feel indecisive about what to keep and what to throw.
- Have a go at a jigsaw, crossword, sudoko, wordsearch or something similar. Great for trying to distract yourself and to feel like you are keeping your brain healthy and functioning.
- Make use of memory aids. For example, a diary, wall calendar, lists, post-it notes, visual prompts (eg if books need taken back to the library, put them beside the front door to remind yourself), reminders on your mobile phone, send emails and texts to yourself, and so on. This will help to counter your poor memory and concentration, at least a little.
- Try simple braintraining or reaction-time types of games or apps on your tablet or phone.
- Listen to music or play an instrument if you have one.
- Reach out to trusted friends and family for support. For example, visit someone, invite someone round, do something for someone, buy someone a present, ask someone you trust for a cuddle, write a text, email or letter, or make a phonecall. You may feel awful / embarrassed / humiliated / negative in all sorts of ways when in the

company of others, but also remember that **your feelings do not define you**, and that most people you know are likely to want to help you.
- At the same time, be aware that a minority of people may shun you, feel neutral about your plight, or just not be equipped to help. Unfortunately I suppose the harsh truth is that this is part of life, and we generally do better when we accept that we cannot be friends with everyone, and others are not perfect. Low self-esteem and depression can lose you friends, or diminish your friendships, there is no point in denying that. But hopefully in the long-run you will be left with quality ahead of quantity in terms of friendships.
- Reaching out can also include looking up helpful, moderated forums on the internet (eg www.patient.co.uk/discussionforums/mental health/depression). You will likely discover that people tend to dwell on their problems excessively on these forums. If you choose to contribute, you might find it helpful to mainly post constructive solution-focussed information and advice, emphasising what you are doing to help yourself, while minimising unhelpful rumination about your negative feelings. This helps you, and it helps others too.
- Attend a local self-help group (eg through Action on Depression in Scotland, Depression Alliance / MIND in England and Wales or Aware-NI in Northern Ireland).
- Help out a local voluntary group, doing non-threatening activities, however you define them.
- Complete a thought record when a negative thought becomes particularly bothersome (see chapter 5). See this as similar to coughing when you get something stuck in your throat, or adjusting the needle on an old record player if the record sticks. You are filling out a thought record to help you to "unstick your mind". Then, importantly, act on your balanced conclusion, which will usually be more helpful than acting on your extreme and unhelpful "hot thought". Again, this is **often difficult to do, but not impossible**.
- Write a poem.
- Paint or draw a picture.
- Sewing, knitting, crochet, or something similarly craft-related.
- Make a model eg airfix.

- Watch TV or listen to the radio (but do this sparingly as both are passive activities, and remember if watching the news that the media tend to focus on the negative, which also increases the risk of slipping into rumination).
- If you want to keep in touch with the news, it's probably better to stick to newspapers or online sources. You have more control this way and you can be more selective in what you read.
- Go to the cinema (usually an activity that is not too socially threatening).
- Go swimming and/or maybe a sauna or steam room.
- Go to a museum or art gallery, and even if you cannot take much in, or fully appreciate your surroundings, set yourself a simple challenge like counting the number of paintings.
- Play a simple board game, dominoes, draughts, patience, whatever you think might be helpful.
- Yoga or Progressive Muscle Relaxation (PMR).
- Guided Visual Imagery.
- SAD light therapy.
- Mindfulness Meditation.
- Read short magazine articles or easy fiction when in the initial stages of recovery. This could involve visiting your local library.
- Buy something affordable and nice for yourself.
- Relax in a warm bath.
- Have a massage or other affordable self-care treat.
- Try to walk tall, even if only in your own company.
- Remind yourself that you did not choose to be this way, it is an illness, and it will pass. If surviving becomes really, really difficult, there are other options and treatments that can help. Try to cling onto hope with your fingernails.
- Bear in mind the Catch 22's (chapter 1) of Depression, which reminds us that recovery from depression is made difficult (but not impossible) by all of the symptoms of depression. But there is always a little bit of wriggle-room to chip away at.

It is tricky to tell the difference between doing a reasonable amount of non-threatening activity and doing too much or too little. You will get it wrong at times, you will overly-tire yourself, or not do enough, but we all have the right to take calculated risks, and we all have the right to make mistakes (see assertive rights below). Don't be too hard on yourself, dust yourself down and re-assess what you can cope with for the rest of today.

The above makes an assumption that your depressive illness has caused you to miss work and you are at home, trying to fill your day. This is often the case. However, it may well be that you are just about able to soldier on at work, and you value this because you see your work and its inherent structure and activity as meaningful and beneficial for you. If this is the case, then I would suggest focussing on the core duties of your job and not trying to do extra. You could speak with a trusted manager and negotiate lighter duties, working from home at least some of the time, or being granted extended deadlines for projects. It is usually in their interest to have you doing something, rather than off work doing nothing. If your employer or manager is not decent, or if you simply cannot cope, then arrange to see your GP and they will usually sign you off for a while so can you can recover at home. He / she will also act as gatekeeper for any NHS or private referral to be made on your behalf.

Official Guidance

Alongside the ad hoc list of stuff that has worked for me, there is a huge amount of evidence-based guidance out there on constructive behaviour change. Ideas can be gleaned from the SIGN Guidelines in Scotland. The Scottish Intercollegiate Guidelines Network (SIGN) - a part of NHS Quality Improvement Scotland - regularly publishes updates to its guidelines for management of chronic health conditions. SIGN Guideline 114 concerns itself with the "Non-Pharmaceutical Management of Depression in Adults". It was last updated in 2010 by a large team of respected academics and clinicians. It can be seen in context alongside a similar guideline for the whole of the UK, namely NICE Guideline CG90.

In terms of psychological therapies to seek out, the SIGN Guideline strongly recommends Behavioural Activation (BA) (a fancy name for what we are discussing in this chapter), individual CBT (mentioned in chapter 5) and Interpersonal Therapy (IPT). Recent evidence from IAPT (Increasing Access to Psychological Therapies) in England and

Wales, stresses IPT as particularly useful for depression. IPT has a strong behavioural slant, emphasising the importance of pushing yourself to reach out to maintain or expand social networks. It promotes making best use of your social resources if you like. SIGN also supports Mindfulness-Based CBT in a group setting, problem-solving therapy, and short-term psychodynamic psychotherapy once you can concentrate better. In terms of self-help options it strongly recommends guided self-help (accessed via the NHS or sometimes the voluntary sector, and usually provided by an Assistant Psychologist) and computerised CBT (eg the aforementioned www.livinglifetothefull.com, www.beatingtheblues.co.uk and others). Last but not least it mentions support for structured and regular exercise.

Remember that in the midst of a depressive episode you are likely not well enough to engage in psychological therapy. Stick to "battoning down the hatches and waiting out the storm" in terms of your thoughts, and chipping away at your depression in terms of non-threatening BA. I think the self-help strategies may be worth a try (guided self-help, computerised CBT and exercise) when you are ill, and of course there are therapists who specialise in BA who could support you through an acute episode. But I would refrain from launching into any of the other recommended psychological therapies until your concentration recovers to a decent enough level. Best to leave the talking therapies till later, all of which have strong evidence for helping to preventing relapse.

A very important caveat to the talking therapies having a strong evidence base is that a person does best when they "fit well" with their therapist. Some scientists would call this the importance of "operator variables". That is, if you get on with your therapist in an amicable way and feel like he or she can help you, then you will probably work successfully together (providing they know their stuff well enough). If you would prefer a therapist of the same sex, or your gut instinct says you are not well matched, then you have every right to ask to see someone else.

Unhelpful or High Cost Behaviour

Alcohol can be part of a person's diet (see chapter 4), but the act of drinking it is a behaviour, so it is important to also consider it here. As said, it is not recommended in general, as it is a Central Nervous System depressant. I would certainly avoid it completely when in the throes of the illness (the same goes for other significant mind-altering substances). When well again, the exception might be to drink minimally or in moderation when in the company of trusted, mutually respected friends and / or family. This is an individual decision as we are all very different in terms of metabolism and how alcohol affects us. Drinking certainly comes with a disclaimer. It can oil the wheels of a good social time together. But it can be very problematic in terms of doing or saying things you will later regret, or – just as potentially damaging – passively NOT doing or saying things you will later regret. In other words, it can increase the likelihood of thinking and feeling negatively about yourself, which can trigger depression. So alcohol is not ruled out, but we fully acknowledge that we are taking a significant risk if we choose to drink. In my experience often this risk will backfire, as it tends to strengthen my default setting (collection of core beliefs) towards self-deprecation, putting myself down, being overly-modest and so on. From a wider perspective we can also see alcohol as simply another stressor on our system (see Stress Vulnerability Model, chapter 5), increasing the chance of relapse.

It is very tempting to blame others for our depression. Try not to. Try to take ownership and be assertive where necessary (see below). Our pasts may have been difficult, others may have been at fault in the way they treated us, but we won't get very far if we dwell and ruminate (interestingly, a wise former colleague of mine once highlighted that the word ruminate is derived from the word ruminant, which describes the digestive systems of animals such as cows, who process grass very slowly through 3 stomachs in a loop system, regurgitating and chewing repeatedly – really quite apt as an analogy for our tendency to unhelpfully "chew" over our thoughts.).

We do better when we endeavour to live in the moment, be assertive with others, and try to understand, accept and forgive those who have transgressed against us.

We will discuss assertiveness in detail down below. Regarding **understanding, accepting and forgiving,** it is helpful to **understand** as best we can why people in our past behaved the way they did. If the person or people involved are still alive, this might involve asking them direct questions about their behaviour with a constructive mindset (ie not aiming to assassinate their character). If they are dead or not contactable, you might still be able to do some research on their lives to shed light on their actions towards you (eg ask relatives or friends). Hopefully this leads to **acceptance** that while what has happened cannot be changed, there is room to revise your interpretation of events. Ultimately it is then in our interest to move on to **forgive**, because this will help us feel better about ourselves in the long-run (you can see why most religions promote forgiveness). For more on understanding, accepting and forgiving, see the previously mentioned book "Manhood" by Steve Biddulph, specifically the chapter on "Fixing it With Your Father" (I believe the same principles apply to all relationships, especially also between daughters and mothers).

In my case I swung between an initial idealised recollection of my father, to a bitter and resentful one. I then did a lot of research on his life and the illness of alcoholism and I have generally been at peace with him since. At the same time the process of understanding, accepting and forgiving is one which often requires repeating. To this day I can be at peace with my father one week and lapse into slight bitterness and resentment the next, which requires me to re-commit to the process of understanding, accepting and forgiving. Essentially he was an imperfect human being, just like us all. He also suffered from a severe chronic addictive illness. It does not serve me well to be bitter.

Assertive Skills

Being assertive is about staying as calm as possible, and being open, honest, direct and respectful with others. It's about staying balanced. As Rudyard Kipling said in his famous poem "If", sometimes it's about "keeping your head when all about you are losing theirs." Most of us know how to be assertive, but don't do it all the time. Some of us struggle to be assertive in most situations. There will be reasons why you struggle to be assertive, most probably (but not always) from childhood. **But we can all learn to be more consistently assertive.**

If we see assertiveness as being at the mid-point of a continuum (see figure 8), we can see passive behaviour as being at one end, and aggressive behaviour at the other. Passive behaviour usually only leads to pent up anger and bitterness, while aggressive behaviour often results in feelings of guilt and regret. This makes complete sense when we appreciate that passive behaviour gives out the message that "my needs are less important than yours". We bottle up our opinions, feelings, rights and needs at great risk to ourselves (especially with regards to depression). In the short-term we avoid confrontation and this may reduce anxiety, but in the long-run we significantly lower our sense of self-esteem. Meanwhile being aggressive pushes home the opinion that "my needs are more important than yours". We ram our opinions, feelings, rights and needs down other people's throats with no respect for theirs. In the short-term this may help a person feel powerful, but aggressive behaviour usually leads to guilt and shame and a loss of friendships (and positive reinforcement) in time. Of note, like too much passivity, consistent aggression can also significantly lower your self-esteem over the longer-term.

Figure 8 : Continuum of passive, assertive, aggressive. Aim for the middle ground.

[------------------------------------/------------------------------------]
Passive   Assertive   Aggressive

Now, I have attended both an Assertive Skills group as a patient, and facilitated Assertive Skills groups at different times in my career, so I can fully appreciate how crucial assertiveness is in terms of keeping us psychologically well. I have worked hard myself to overcome tendencies to passive behaviour, with occasional verbal aggression spilling out when I take the passivity too far. I have discovered that this pattern of behaviour is far from unique and is also far from helpful. Fortunately I have learned to become more assertive, and this consistent assertiveness has lead to higher self-esteem on the whole. The aim is always to ask for what you want or need, be prepared to persist and repeat yourself, but also be prepared to accept compromise (often this can be a "win-win" for both parties). It is simply a balanced approach which respects both or all parties present.

Let me be clear on consistent passive behaviour. The plain truth is this : every time you suppress a response in order to please another or others you run the risk of damaging your own mental health and tipping yourself over into clinical depression. Too often this has been in the mix when I have relapsed. You are essentially putting others' needs ahead of your own, treating them as more important than you (see figure 9).

Figure 9 : Stick men diagram illustrating passive, assertive and aggressive

Behaviour   **Message conveyed**

Passive   Your needs are more important than mine, I feel smaller in comparison

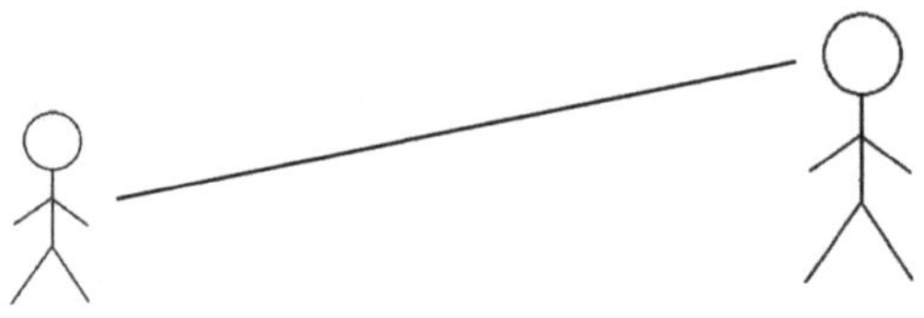

Aggressive   My needs are more important than yours, I feel bigger in comparison

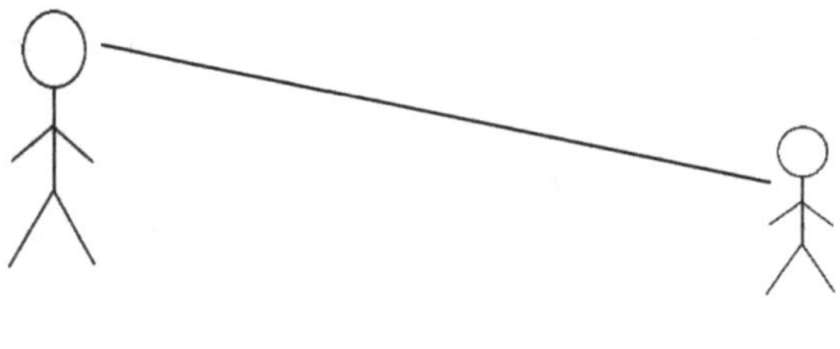

Assertive   My needs are equal to yours.

Here are the fundamentals of what it is to be assertive :

- Standing up for yourself confidently, sometimes despite how you feel inside.
- Being open, honest and direct.
- Getting your opinions and feelings across to others.
- Seeing your opinions and feelings as valid, while respecting others opinions and feelings.
- Doing all of the above calmly and respectfully as far as possible, but reserving the right to express anger appropriately.
- Forgiving yourself when you don't get it right every time.

This "attitude" of assertiveness is underpinned by our **Assertive Rights**, as follows :

I have the right to :

1. **Recognise my own needs as an individual.** That is, separate from what might be expected of me in roles such as "husband", "wife", "son", "daughter", "girlfriend", "boyfriend", "brother", "sister" or "employee".
2. **Respect myself.** Respect who I am and what I do, and expect to be treated with respect by others.
3. **Allow myself to make mistakes.** Recognise that this is normal.

4. **Allow myself to change my mind.** I can choose to do this and it is ok to do so.
5. **Not know everything.** I can say "I don't know" or "I don't understand".
6. **Make clear "I" statements.** Own your thoughts and feelings. For example, "I disagree with your opinion on that." "No, I don't want to do that."
7. **Ask for what I want.** Rather than hoping someone will read my mind and guess what I want.
8. **Ask for "thinking it over time."** Rather than jump into making a hasty decision, you can usually ask for some time to think it over. For example, "I will let you know my decision by the end of the week," or "Let me get back to you on that once I've had a think".
9. **Allow myself to enjoy my successes.** Give yourself a pat on the back. This is not the same as being boastful. Be open to sharing your successes with others.
10. **Recognise that I am not responsible for the behaviour of other adults.** Too often we carry misplaced guilt around on our shoulders.
11. **Respect other people and their right to also be assertive.** Better that they are open, honest, respectful and direct with us.
12. **Make intuitive statements.** I can voice hunches or theories that have no logical basis and which I do not have to justify.
13. **Make my own decisions.** And to live with the consequences.
14. **Sometimes be alone and independent.**

(Williams et.al, 2000)

Adopting these rights and putting them into practice, **while difficult (not impossible)**, involves learning different assertive strategies, including :

1. **"Broken Record".** Repeat your position over and over again, calmly and clearly. Be persistent and patient. An example of this could be when you take something back to a shop and request your money back. Or if someone asks you for money and you don't want to lend it to him/her.

2. **Saying No.** Just say it and repeat if necessary. Be polite but firm. No need to apologise or give long-winded excuses. You have the right to say no. Remember that in the long run it is better to be honest rather than breed bitterness and resentment within yourself.
3. **Scripting.** Planning ahead for a potentially difficult interaction with someone. Doing this in your mind or jotting it down on paper. What do you want to say and how are you going to say it ?
4. **Giving and receiving compliments assertively.** Don't be afraid to give compliments where you feel they are due. And if you are on the receiving end of one, accept it. As a minimum, just say thanks. Don't bat it back or minimise it, as this deprives you of the chance to bolster your self-esteem and is not fair on the compliment-giver.
5. **Giving and receiving criticism assertively.** In terms of giving criticism, be open, honest and direct in your critique of the behaviour of the person. No need to assassinate their character. Regarding receiving criticism assertively, listen to what is being said and either : a) agree it is 100% fair criticism ; b) accept some of it as fair but not all of it, or ; c) disagree with all of the criticism calmly but firmly.
6. **Giving and receiving apologies assertively.** Regarding giving an apology, this involves being courageous and apologising for what you feel is appropriate in a given situation. That might be a whole apology, or a part-apology where you apologise for what you think you did wrong, but also carefully communicate what you do not think you need to apologise for. Be careful not to put your whole self down when apologising, making it clear that your behaviour was out of order, not you as a person ("I behaved like an idiot" rather than "I am an idiot"). In terms of receiving an apology, make it clear that you accept it or don't accept it (depending on whether it was communicated to you assertively).

So there is a strong argument that, once we are well again, learning to behave assertively can reduce our chances of relapse (see "Assert Yourself" by Gael Lindenfield for a more detailed guide). But this book is mainly about helping people to survive an episode of depressive illness, so I also want to briefly look at assertiveness from another perspective. When in the throes of the illness itself, we can also use the principles of assertiveness training inwardly, on our thinking.

Assertiveness Applied Inwardly

We don't have to discuss much here. I'm simply talking about applying assertive skills to ourselves. It makes common sense. If we can talk to ourselves with respect, be firm yet fair, be patient, be persistent, and stay as calm as possible, we have a far better chance of getting better, quicker. If we can stand up assertively to the bully that is depression, we can defeat it over time. Remember that old rhyme from school : "Sticks and stones may break my bones, but names can never hurt me". That's the kind of attitude you can benefit from. The "lying bully" of depression can rabbit on, but you don't need to take him/her so seriously. If we are passive in the face of depression, we risk giving in and it overwhelming us. If we respond aggressively to it, we can tire ourselves out, run ourselves down and have no fight left for the long battle ahead. Being persistently assertive with ourselves really is the only way forward. As the front cover illustrates, it's about chipping away at your depression doggedly and determinedly. Combine this attitude with the advice in chapters 3, 4 and 5, and you will get there.

Chapter 7 : Other Treatments

Hospital Admission

In cases of severe clinical depression, admission to psychiatric hospital is only occasionally necessary, usually through the NHS in the UK, or privately if you have insurance or can afford it (into somewhere like the Priory). A religious or spiritual retreat may be an option – although these are options I know little about. Most retreats cost money ; only a minority are free to access. This may be worth an internet search.

Admission to hospital tends to happen only when a person is so deeply depressed that they start to feel persecuted by delusional (false) thoughts or beliefs, or they may be so sluggish and demotivated that they are neglecting their own self-care to an extent considered harmful. In other words there is concern over them becoming a danger to themselves, or very rarely, to others (sometimes described as psychotic depression). Such a person may be able to remain at home providing there is an effective support network of family, community nurses and psychiatrist. Hospital admission is also possible if you are experiencing suicidal thoughts and have formulated some sort of plan – if this is the case you may need protecting from yourself. Very rarely a depressed person requires sectioned under the Mental Health Act because they are so ill they cannot see that they need cared for.

Hopefully you will not require admission to hospital. A school of thought exists that the last place a depressed person needs to be is surrounded by other mentally ill people in the often noisy and stressful environment of an acute psychiatric ward. It may also be that, paradoxically, psychiatric hospital provides too much help for some depressed inpatients. They can become over-dependent and institutionalised pretty quickly.

It is certainly worth considering other options. Could you be supported a little more at home eg with friends and relatives rallying round, and/or visits from members of your local Crisis Support Team or Community Mental Health Team (CMHT)? Could you stay at relatives or friends for a while? Could you tap into a local self-help group eg run under the umbrella of Depression Alliance / MIND or

Action on Depression? Could a Social Worker, Welfare Benefits Adviser or local Citizens Advice Bureau help with financial worries you may have? If you think the answer is yes to any of these questions, ask your GP to refer you to the local CMHT, if she/he hasn't already done so.

If you would prefer to minimise contact with statutory services, is there a local voluntary organisation which provides support, drop-ins or befriending services? [eg Scottish Association for Mental Health (SAMH), Carr-Gomm, SANE or MIND].

However, your illness may be so powerful and your options so limited, that you might have to consider hospital admission. Or, your illness might not be extremely severe, but you are lacking in support from family and friends and you are feeling really discouraged, struggling to stay afloat. Maybe you have never really learned how to look after yourself, and now that you are in the midst of this depression you really can't cope with the daily basics of keeping clean, and eating and drinking sufficiently. Ultimately, the hospital option is there as a last resort if you are really struggling to cope.

Whichever way someone ends up being admitted, the basic truth of the matter is that if you do require to be cared for in hospital, it is a bit of a lottery as to the experience you will have. Having trained and worked in psychiatric hospitals, I know the variations between hospitals - and between wards within hospitals - in the standards of care.

Part of this is related to the environment of most acute wards. The staff tend to be somewhat removed (physically, and sometimes emotionally) from the patients a lot of the time, in the duty room, taking a barrage of phonecalls, writing up notes, or talking among themselves. And the patient population in the average acute ward tends to be a a mix of people exhibiting psychotic, manic, depressive or no significant symptoms (the latter being the people who are on the mend, or maybe shouldn't have been there in the first place). If you have never been in an acute ward, and you are severely depressed, at first glance it is potentially a scary place to be.

However, on the plus side, once a person settles in, she/he would most likely benefit from the 'asylum' factor. That is, you would be in a relatively safe place, sheltered, warm, and with reasonable food on offer. Surrounded by people who, on the whole, empathise with your predicament.

There are many decent, dedicated and caring staff who work in the acute wards. Hopefully the depressed patient will be assigned one as their keyworker, or come into regular contact with the best staff. On good wards this will also involve participation in scheduled activities, run by group nurses or occupational therapists. These therapeutic activities might include relaxation groups, support groups, art, woodwork, gardening, and such like.

It is also true that a lot of the informal chatting and 'supporting' is done by the student nurses, care assistants and agency staff. Do not underestimate their importance in helping you to recover ; they often have more time to talk, are more motivated, less consumed by the paperwork side of things, and less likely to be feeling cynical or hassled with full-time caring. Furthermore, some people would say that it is talking and empathising with fellow patients that really helps them to get better (in some instances this may be underplaying the role of medication and staff interventions, but it is some people's perception, so it is worth mentioning, and may well be true in some cases).

Finally, the depressed patient benefits enormously if he/she is assigned a good psychiatrist who has the time and patience to listen, work collaboratively, and prescribe appropriate medication (not too much and not too little). Ideally they will focus more on **what has happened to you rather than what is wrong with you**, but in reality psychiatrists may be lacking in the time needed to do this.

Electroconvulsive Therapy (ECT)

If a severely depressed person has been in hospital for some time, and is not tolerating or responding well to anti-depressants, a last resort for treatment is sometimes electro-convulsive therapy, or ECT. Occasionally someone may be brought in from home for outpatient ECT.

In 2001 I worked in an ECT treatment room. It was my first Mental Health Nursing post after qualifying. It was a position in a Day Unit in Barrow-in-Furness, Cumbria. My job was mainly about co-facilitating group therapy, from assertive skills to relaxation to communication skills. I only found out that ECT was part of my job remit during my first week.

At first I was a little worried and hesitant. During my RMN training I had only ever accompanied one patient from an acute ward to ECT. I had not witnessed what had gone on behind the closed doors. I had read a fair bit about it, but what I had read had been largely negative. Or maybe I should say, most of what I took in was largely negative, because I tended to ignore anything positive about it. Most of us have this preconception about ECT, often related to the 1975 film with Jack Nicholson, "One Flew over the Cuckoo's Nest".

Some facts (based on my own experience and wider research) :

- ECT is an effective last-resort treatment for medication-resistant and psychotherapy-resistant severe clinical depression. A very small number of very ill patients are administered the treatment nowadays (around 0.2% of those who suffer from depression in any one year).

- Numerous studies over the past 60 years have demonstrated ECT's effectiveness. In uncomplicated cases of severe major depression, at least 80% of patients respond favourably.

- It no longer gets foisted onto people. This was a genuine worry up to the 1960's, when 'troublesome' patients were sometimes 'punished' for their behaviour with a dose of it. However, regulations have been very tight in the UK, the EU and other western nations for some time now. Informed consent must be given by the patient ; a second doctor's opinion must also be sought. The second doctor should be on the Mental Welfare Commission (separate bodies for England + Wales and Scotland) and from outwith the local area.

- Patients are given a full medical examination beforehand for other medical disorders which might increase the risk associated with having ECT. Over-55's require an ECG and x-rays on top of this. Recent heart problems or stroke would rule someone out. So would the taking of certain medications which may act as a barrier to the general anaesthetic.

- A full explanation should be given prior to each and every treatment, and repeated where necessary, given the likelihood that the patient has depression-related problems with concentration and memory. Treatment is usually in the morning, so fasting from midnight is required.

- In one sense ECT is no more dangerous than minor surgery under general anaesthesia (like day-surgery, it is sometimes given on an out-patient basis). Unlike the disturbing scene in "One Flew over the Cuckoo's Nest" where the lead character convulses violently on the treatment table, the modern method of administering ECT is much more humane. The patient is given a short-acting general anaesthetic followed by an injection of muscle relaxant. The psychiatrist administers the treatment ; the anaesthetist delivers the anaesthetic and muscle-relaxant, and keeps the patient oxygenated ; and nurses reassure the patient in the build-up and during recovery. The patient is 'under' for about 10 minutes in total.

- The general picture during the treatment is that the psychiatrist places the electrodes at precise locations either side of the patient's skull. These electrodes have wet conducting gel applied evenly over them. The electricity is passed between the electrodes in a brief controlled series of pulses. The patient's body stiffens slightly. The face tightens slightly more. This happens over the course of a second or two. Then the induced fit starts. It lasts for between 10-40 seconds. Thanks mainly to the muscle-relaxant it is pretty low-key, and painless for the unconscious patient concerned ; certainly not the way I had imagined it to be. The patient wears loose fitting clothing, and jewellery and glasses are removed. Any dentures are also removed. A mouth-guard is worn in case the tongue is bitten.

- Essentially what ECT does is to artificially induce a epileptiform seizure. The amount of electricity passed between the skull is actually very small. It varies from person to person depending on their seizure "threshold" ; that is the carefully calculated minimum dose of electricity required to stimulate a seizure. It is reassuring for some to know that they are not being blasted with a 'one-size-fits-all' super-voltage ; instead the amount they receive is tailored to their individual make-up. Also, the amount of electricity that ultimately enters the brain is only a fraction of what is applied to the scalp.

- The number of treatments administered is usually somewhere between 6 and 8, sometimes up to 12. This normally happens twice a week over the course of 4 - 6 weeks.

- There are side-effects. Headache following treatment is common. Paracetemol is usually effective. Muscle soreness, nausea and confusion can be a problem. In many ways, not dissimilar to the aftermath of someone having a 'natural' epileptic seizure. However, most contentious is the effect on memory. Over the course of ECT it may become difficult for patients to remember newly-learned information. There may also be problems with memories of events that happened in the days, weeks and months prior to ECT. Sometimes it is hard to tease out what the depression-related memory problem is, and what might have been caused by the ECT. Whatever the case, for the majority, these difficulties usually clear up in the weeks after treatment finishes. Some even report an improvement in memory due to ECT's ability to help lift the symptoms of severe depression. Research has never found strong evidence for ECT-associated brain damage, but the possibility cannot be ruled out.

This is a very brief summary of what ECT is about. Hopefully it is a reasonably objective summary, but cognitive dissonance on my part is obviously a possibility. That is, I might be defending the procedure more than it deserves because I was involved in the administration of the process myself. There is a huge amount of literature out there on the subject. Ultimately it is an unorthodox, risky procedure. But then, being severely depressed is a hugely risky business too. If you are desperately ill and have been suffering for months with no respite, if your psychiatrist suggests it, you are probably best to at least consider. At the same time if you are severely depressed you will be lacking your usual decision-making ability, which makes it hugely difficult for you to decide. Suffice to say it does appear to help a lot of people. It may be scary for you to contemplate it, but if it may help to end the torture of your depression, perhaps it's worth a try. As I have witnessed, ECT is administered very carefully these days and it is proven to be effective ; it is certainly not the kind of barbaric treatment portrayed by Hollywood in the 1970's.

That said, statistically it is unlikely that you are considering, or being considered for ECT. As was mentioned the numbers involved are very small. However, if you are, again it is worth stressing that it is your choice alone (unless you are being held under a section of the Mental Health Act, which is uncommon for a depressed person). You might want to tough it out and wait till the depression lifts, which it most likely will sooner or later. But can you tolerate the wait for that ?

There are some other physical treatments used more rarely than ECT. Neurosurgical procedures and deep brain stimulation are only considered in the most extreme of cases, where everything else has failed.

(For what its worth, I have never had ECT and I am glad that I have not. But if I ever became ill again for 3 months or more, I would certainly consider it.)

Transcranial Magnetic Stimulation (TMS)

A possible alternative to ECT is repeated Transcranial Magnetic Stimulation (rTMS). This is a less complicated and less traumatic procedure for the patient to experience. It is immediately safer on four counts, in that : 1) there is no need for seizure induction, general anaesthetic or muscle relaxant ; 2) the patient remains conscious throughout, usually sitting upright and able to move and interact with staff ; 3) cognitive side-effects are either absent or minimal ; and 4) the patient can immediately return to daily activities following the procedure.

There are two major similarities between ECT and TMS : both induce neuronal depolarisation and both appear similar in effectiveness in depression. However, TMS achieves this in a more focussed way.

Powerful magnetic fields are applied to the brain in rapid succession, usually to the front left cortex on the top of the head ('left dorsolateral prefrontal' in neurological language). The magnetic activity is usually induced by figure-of-eight-shaped insulated rubber coils of copper wire, held just above the patient's head. The magnetic fields pass relatively unobstructed through bone and other tissue with only minor discomfort. It seems like this - in a similar way to ECT and antidepressants - can help to increase blood flow to important mood-associated areas of the brain, and improve communication between brain cells.

The experience of the treatment for the patient is unusual but generally comfortable. In order to establish a baseline for treatment, the intensity of stimulations are increased from a low level upwards, until movement or twitching is observed in the hand muscles (usually thumb). This is done because the primary motor cortex of the brain is the most sensitive to stimulation. The clinicians can then base the treatment proper on that 'threshold dose' (similar in principle to the seizure threshold calculated for ECT).

When the localised electric current is induced by the magnetic field (that is, the treatment starts), the patient feels a noticeable but gentle 'tapping' at the focal point. Not unlike a very small hammer being gently tapped against your skull. The strength and rate of the stimulus varies. That is, the tapping may be faster or slower, and involve more or less electric current, depending on the severity of the depressive symptoms. The gap between 'bursts of tapping' also varies. In total, a treatment usually lasts for between 10-20 minutes.

Although not common, possible side-effects include : local discomfort relating to nerve and muscle stimulation in the scalp ; slight pain relating to heat emitted by the coil ; tension headaches ; short-term cognitive side-effects ; and a short-term 'acoustic' artefact (that is, the sound of tapping continuing in your mind afterwards). There is also a very small risk of provoked seizure, less than 1%. Significantly, no permanent memory or other cognitive deficits have been reported.

Unfortunately at the time of writing the options in the UK for rTMS are limited. The Nightingale Hospital in London offers a private service for people with treatment-resistant depression, using a new

"H"-type coil, which is reported to stimulate deeper regions of the limbic system as well as the more superficial cortical areas targeted by the figure-of-eight coil. The London Psychiatry Centre also offers the treatment, which was recently endorsed by the NICE Guidelines and Healthcare Improvement Scotland (December, 2015).

Again, for what it is worth, I have some experience of TMS. Back in 1998 while a Mental Health Nursing student in Edinburgh, I responded to an advert for volunteers for TMS research at the Royal Edinburgh Hospital (£25 being quite handy when you're a student). Following a particularly difficult early shift on one of the nearby acute wards, I went along to participate. My mood was vulnerable. While the dose, frequency and gaps between pulses were experimental - therefore lower than would be used for treatment - I found the whole procedure to be fairly stress-free. The tapping on the skull was mildly irritating after a few minutes but that was about the only discomfort. Most vivid to me now is the Verbal Fluency Test (VFT) that I was assigned to do before and after the treatment. The VFT involves thinking of as many words as possible beginning with a random letter in one minute. This was one of a few measures employed in the experiment. As I say, I had had a difficult early shift and was on a bit of a (natural) downer when I attended for the procedure. So I was a bit slowed up and distracted for the first go of the VFT. I struggled a little to think of many words. Then I had to do the same for two more letters. However, when I repeated the task after the TMS it was a different story. The words positively flowed into my head and I came up with significantly more than before.

This, of course, is purely anecdotal evidence for TMS. I was down but not clinically depressed at the time ; the procedure would no doubt be a different proposition for someone in the midst of the illness. And I received an experimental dose ; a treatment dose may be harder to sit through. But it does suggest that there is at least the possibility of an infinitely more comfortable and equally effective 'last-resort' treatment for depression compared with relatively crude ECT.

More recently an alternative to traditional rTMS has arrived on the scene. Low-Field Magnetic Stimulation (LFMS) claims to lead to immediate and substantial mood improvement, using magnetic fields that are a fraction of the strength, but at a higher frequency than the electromagnetic fields used in TMS. Patients are required to lie down and place their heads inside a device not unlike a miniaturised MRI scanner. Researchers working at McLean Hospital and linked to Harvard Medical School in the USA report patients experiencing quick relief and less side-effects compared with medication and ECT (2014). They argue that LFMS could be used alone or in combination with medication as a rapidly acting treatment for depression.

It puzzles me why rTMS and and LFMS are not available more widely on the NHS in the UK. The FDA in America approved it for treatment resistant depression in 2008, but at the time of writing - other than a few private clinics - only one NHS Trust in Northamptonshire offers it on our health service. Perhaps in time, as the evidence builds up, it will become more available and ECT will be phased out. The signs are promising : the National Institute for Clinical Excellence (NICE, 2014) recently approved it for the treatment and prevention of migraine.

Chapter 8 : Staying Well, New Treatments and Final Thoughts

"Please grant me the serenity
to accept the things I cannot change,
the courage to change the things I can,
and the wisdom to know the difference."

Alcoholics Anonymous, Al-Anon, Gamblers Anonymous, Narcotics Anonymous and other "Anonymous" groups (and applicable to everyone)

"Just because you think a thought, it does not mean to say that it is true or meaningful".

Obvious in a sense, but very important all the same. Not sure who said this first. I say this a lot, or words very similar.

Staying Well

In terms of preventing relapse, I think most of us would do ok if we lived our lives according to the above quotes. In terms of a little more detail on top of these broad statements, I believe you can keep consistently well if you do some or all of the following :

- Endeavour to be more authentic and **assertive** with others as much as you can, when appropriate. I say "when appropriate", because there are times in life when standing your ground and being assertive is not recommended. For example, when faced with a potentially violent situation, you are usually better off trying to get out of the situation. However, for the most part, risk of relapse is generally increased if you clam up, choose the path of least resistance, keep quiet to keep the peace, and other such passive behaviour. Likewise if you lose it, shout and scream, and other such aggressive behaviour, you also increase your chances of slipping back.

- Regarding **medication**, if there is benefit, or at least hope of some benefit, then take your prescribed medication on a regular basis at regular times.
- Eat a mood-promoting healthy **diet**, including probiotics and omega-3's. It does not have to be perfect, but it is worth making some extra effort.
- **Hydrate** yourself adequately. Remember the body is 80% water so you need a decent amount of fluid every day. The more water the better, minimising sugary drinks, and aiming for 1.5 – 2 litres as a ballpark figure.
- Keep to a routine in terms of **personal hygiene**, to a standard you are content with.
- Minimise your **alcohol** intake (this can be a huge risk factor).
- Keep reasonably fit and **active** in order to boost self-esteem.
- Get involved in your **community** or perhaps do some voluntary work.
- Keep learning, perhaps via an evening class or online course.
- Set yourself SMART **goals**. That is short, medium and long-term goals that are specific, measurable, achievable, realistic and timely. Examples could be : I am going to take the dog out for at least one walk every day for half an hour ; I am going to eat at least one piece of fruit and something containing probiotics and tryptophan every day ; I will paint the spare bedroom gradually with two coats of emulsion, one wall at a time, and aim to be finished in 2 days ; I will arrange the painting of the house by the end of the summer ; or I will gradually build up my training to run a 10k next year in May. Whatever suits you.
- **Face your fears**, challenge yourself. Within reason.
- Get into more of a routine. Especially with your **sleep**. If you can, go to bed most nights at around the same time after winding down for an hour, get up at a consistent time, and minimise napping in the day. If you have problems with waking up in the night, don't toss and turn. Instead get up after 20 minutes and do something relaxing in another warm room in the house. When you feel "sleepy-tired" again, return to bed. Repeat as necessary. If you struggle to get off to sleep, stop reading, watching TV and looking at tablets or phones in bed. Treat your bed as being for sleep and sex only. If none of that works, consider the approach of Sleep

Restriction Therapy (SRT), which can be a very effective, last resort, non-pharmacological approach (see work by Professor Colin Espie of Glasgow University).
- Consistently notice, and then either assertively challenge or dismiss, your negative, unhelpful **thinking**.
- Remind yourself that your thoughts do not define you, that you cannot directly control over what jumps into your mind at times, but you do have **choices** once the thoughts are there. Acknowledge that, like everyone, you occasionally think some bizarre, strange, weird, and potentially distressing thoughts. Accept their presence in your mind as pretty normal, but you don't always have to accept their message, or even see such thoughts as meaningful.
- Keep connected with your **social network**, focussing on the positive people you feel most comfortable with. Make the effort to make new, positive friends if opportunities present themselves.
- Be **mindful**. Notice life around you in the moment. Notice shapes, patterns, the rhythm of your breathing, sensations, smells, sounds. Enrol in a mindfulness course or take up yoga or tai chi. Make some time to relax.
- Strive to be aware that depression can hit you anytime, anywhere, no matter how long you have been well for. Like the infamous story in AA folklore, of the severe alcoholic who stopped drinking at the age of 30, got his life and career back on track, and stayed sober until he retired, only to "allow himself" a drink at his retirement do. A vicious relapse ensued and within a year he was dead. Depressive **relapse** is not generally as extreme as that, but the story serves as a reminder of sorts, that once the depressive path has been trodden, there is always a chance that you will unwittingly, habitually, follow its familiar path again (remember the metaphor of the person changing their dog-walking route, p.98).
- If you still have nagging doubts that something is not quite right, examine your **situation** in life. Would you benefit from changing things? For example, does your partnership / marriage need worked on ? Does your job require you to sell some of your integrity every day – if so, can you learn to accept this, or would you be better off changing direction? Are you in debt – if so, can you access some good advice

and manage your finances better? Are you feeling disconnected from your community or nature – can you start new activities to remedy this?

- If you become unwell again, choose to stay **patient** (as far as possible) and engage in non-threatening, anti-depressant activity to keep your self ticking over. Remember the catch-22s : there is always scope to chip away at the depression, no matter how daunting it seems. Remember the ulcer model of depression : ulcers heal up quicker with certain interventions, as does depression. Do some or all of the stuff mentioned in chapters 3-6. Batton down the hatches and see out the storm, which always passes. Remind yourself that no matter how dark it gets, daylight will arrive again.

Not all of the above may apply to you. Take what is useful, leave the rest and add your own strategies as appropriate. Keep an open mind. I always remember a quote by an instructor (Bob) on an Outward Bound course I attended 20 odd years ago : "The mind is like a parachute, it only works properly if it is fully open". You never know where an idea will come from, you never know where or when you will find inspiration. Nature may help. Seeing a 3-legged dog accepting its disability and just getting on with life might motivate you. Or you may feel encouraged by observing a spider patiently rebuild a whole web after the original was blown away. A chat with a friend ; a quote from a TV programme ; a magazine article ; a word, sentence or passage from this or another self-help book ; a random thought ...... be open to all potential sources.

Summarising how to stay well is difficult. In my view the best visual attempt that I have seen is a holistic model we present to attendees at our Stress Management Classes. **The Wellness "5-a-day" Model** (figure 10, next page) illustrates nicely some of what is recommended to stay well.

Figure 10 : The Wellness Model (Ref. Five Ways to Wellbeing, New Economics Foundation, Foresight Report (Dept of Health), and mind.org.uk)

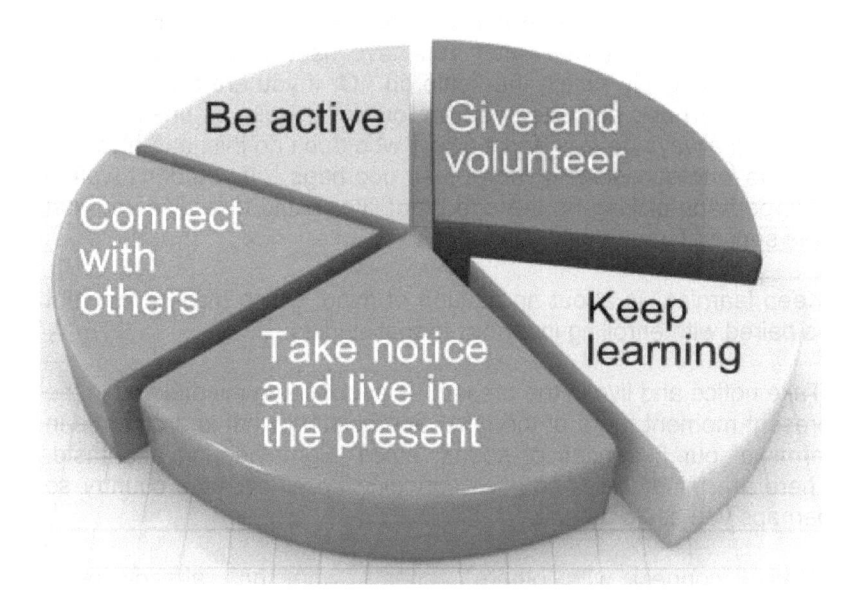

The model is fairly self-explanatory but here are a few points for clarification.

The "Be active" part of the pie is mostly about physical exercise, even if only taking the stairs not the lift. If you can do more than that and get into a regular routine where you are pushing yourself a bit, then even better. Regular exercise releases endorphins and helps us feel better about ourselves, of that there is no doubt. It can help enormously with feeling more in control. It may not have been mentioned in this book as much as some factors, but that does not mean to say that I do not value exercise as important in treating and preventing depression. I would say it is almost a "given" that keeping your body in decent physical shape will also help to improve your self-esteem and stabilise your mental health.

"Give and volunteer" alludes to getting involved more in your local community, perhaps through formal volunteering. It also advocates engaging in more small "random acts of kindness", as they are known in the current parlance. There are thousands of things we could all do in this respect, and of course you don't want to become passive and start doing too much for everyone around you. However, in moderation, examples I can think of include filling up the communal kettle at work after you have used it, so that the next person can simply switch the kettle on. Or if you are a dog walker, bag an extra dog dirt when you are out for a walk, as unfortunately there will always be lazy dog walkers who don't do this, and also dog walkers who occasionally forget their poo bags ! If you don't walk a dog, perhaps picking up the odd bit of litter could help give you that wee sense of community spiritedness.

"Keep learning" is about an attitude of mind, which may or may not be paired with enrolling in further formal studies.

"Take notice and live in the present" is about being mindful and in the present moment more of the time, appreciating what is around us in terms of our 5 senses of sound, smell, sight, hearing and taste. There are mindfulness courses springing up all over the country so perhaps you could try one.

Finally, "connect with others" repeats what has already been mentioned in this book, that positive human company is to be sought out and valued as therapeutic and health-promoting. And that can mean making the effort to talk about yourself as well as listen to others. That is how the natural ebb and flow of (usually mildly competitive) conversation works.

On top of what we have covered here there are literally hundreds of potential treatments and coping options to be found when you search the internet. Evidence may not be as strong for some of these approaches, but that may be simply because not enough good studies have been done yet. The following few examples will likely do you no harm and help to provide distraction, a sense of "taking control back", and possibly even relaxation :

- acupuncture
- massage therapy
- music therapy
- guided imagery

- biofeedback
- aromatherapy
- art therapy
- take a so-called cognitive enhancing supplement like gingko biloba or ginseng
- take the amino-acid tryptophan (the precursor to serotonin) or tyrosine (the precursor to dopamine), 5-HTP or SAMe supplements (consult with your GP first).

I think psychological flexibility is also worth mentioning. If a medication isn't helping, ask for a different one. If a medication is causing problematic side-effects, ask for a different one, or try something non-addictive that may ease the side-effect/s. In my case I am acutely aware that my luck may run out with the lithium, and I may eventually develop side-effects that are too problematic (at the time of writing my benign tremor seems to be worsening slightly, particularly in my left hand). I may ultimately choose to change my medication regime. I may opt to not replace the lithium directly, and see if all of the above strategies (in particular, improved assertiveness and dietary strategies like probiotics and omega-3's) applied more consistently may help me to keep my head above water. But I'll have to get pretty shaky before I consider doing that. I still consider lithium to be my life-saver of sorts.

New Treatments

Biology

Pharmaceutical companies are always looking for new classes of antidepressants, and improved versions of existing ones. For example, escitalopram was introduced to the market around 2002 as a new, supposedly improved version or isomer of well-established citalopram (there is good evidence to back this claim up). Our westernised lifestyles (including our diets ?) seem to be nudging more and more of us into depressive territory, so there is financial gain to be made in alleviating the distress caused by clinical depression. There are many drugs and medical techniques in early and late stages of the research process, all approaching depression and the Central Nervous System (CNS) from slightly different angles. Let's look at some of these :

- Drugs that influence **cortisol**, a stress hormone, are being looked at. Hormones and neurotransmitters influence each other on a two-way street. A drug that manages cortisol levels may help to lift or even prevent depression.
- Low-dose **ketamine** (also used in anaesthesia) is being trialled as a medicine of last resort in patients who have not responded to six separate trials of antidepressants. Traditional intravenous (IV) administration has been looked at, and also more convenient nasal spray and pill form. Possible dissociative side-effects are unpleasant, but an antidote to this is also in development.
- **Vortioxetine (Brintellix)** is a new SSRI licensed by the authorities in the USA in 2013 and the UK in 2015. It is marketed as another option to try in severe depression if two other medications have been tried and failed.
- A combination of the **ghrelin hormone** (a hunger hormone) and a compound known as **P7C3** are being touted as a potentially brand new class of antidepressants, more homeopathic than synthetic.
- **Nerve-growth factor (VGF)** research is in its infancy. This involves the injection of small proteins that develop and maintain nerve cells.
- **MRI scanning** of the brain can increasingly predict who responds well to what type and dose of medication.
- So too can **genetic probability matching** of patient to medication. Simple blood tests are available that assess enzyme activity in the liver and can forecast who will experience more side-effects on one medication compared with another.
- Still more encouraging is **another new blood test** which measures two inflammation biomarkers shown in studies to be linked to a poor response to antidepressants. Levels of both biomarkers above a certain threshold have been shown to 100% predict no response to conventional SSRIs (this makes me think of the useful anti-inflammatory properties inherent in omega-3 fatty acids). This will hopefully lead to less faffing around and suffering, as GPs and patients search for a "personalised" antidepressant as opposed to the almost "pot luck" approach up until now.
- **Microglia cells**, which make up 10% of the cells in our brain, mainly play a role in the immune defence of our CNS. They

fight infectious bacteria and viruses in our brain. Diseased microglia may be involved in causing depression in some of us, as they appear to secrete compounds that cause an inflammatory response (further suggesting a role for anti-inflammatory omega-3 intake).
- **GABA-NAM compounds** in the brain are also being investigated. They reduce the inhibitory messages that are sent via the GABA neurotransmitter, thereby helping the weak excitatory GABA messages to stimulate the brain and lift it out of depression. Research is at a very early stage but there are reports of speedy and dramatic effects in animal studies.
- The peptide **galanin**, found widely in the human nervous system, is thought to play a role in stress, anxiety and depression. Those of us with galanin gene variants seem to be at greater risk of mood problems. Researchers are unclear just how the galanin system influences mood, but there may be potential in the long-term for new antidepressants to target this peptide.
- **Nitrous oxide**, like ketamine, may help lift depression quickly, if only temporarily, until other treatments kick in.
- Rather bizarrely, **botox** injections may also help as an adjunct to an antidepressant. Preventing you from frowning, it seems, can help lift depression. It is not known whether this is because of a biofeedback mechanism ("I can't frown therefore I can't be so depressed") or because other people respond differently to people who don't frown, increasing positive reinforcement from those around you.
- Inflammation has been linked to depression for many years now, so not surprisingly **anti-inflammatory medications** may have a helpful role to play. Ibuprofen, diclofenac and, as we mentioned before, omega-3 supplements are among the options, but make sure to discuss with your GP if you want to add any of these to your medication regime. .

This is all very complex but the overall message is clear. Science is forging ahead looking for better medications with less side-effects. There is always hope for any sufferer that an alternative or newer medication is available, or is on the horizon.

Psychology

Psychological approaches to depression are also constantly evolving. The last 50 years has seen the rise and popularisation of CBT, while the past 20 years has seen the growth of the so-called "third-wave" of cognitive-behavioural therapies, such as : Acceptance and Commitment Therapy (ACT) ; Interpersonal Therapy (IPT) ; Compassion-Focussed Therapy (CFT) ; Mindfulness Based Cognitive Therapy (MBCT) ; Schema Therapy ; Cognitive Analytic Therapy (CAT) and Cognitive Behavioural Analysis System of Psychotherapy (CBASP) for treatment-resistant individuals. You can never underestimate the power and effectiveness of sitting down with someone knowledgeable, empathic, caring and neutral to discuss your problems constructively. Also utilising the trans-diagnostic CBT tool, the thought record, which can help you to take control and balance your thinking out. The "top-down" can be just as effective, if not more so, than the "bottom-up".

The Future

Critically, the future for depression treatment is optimistic. As discussed, there is increasing choice and availability in terms of useful psychological therapy, and there is a drive towards more individual, tailor-made medications and treatments, involving less in the way of side-effects. Add in the recent developments in nutritional medicine and there are even more grounds for positivity. Perhaps we have hugely underestimated the effect on our bodies and minds of changes in our diet over the past 300 years. In evolutionary terms 300 years is the blink of an eye, yet industrialisation and the move from agrarian to urban society has driven most of us to consume more omega-6 in the form of cereal-based foods, excess sugar and saturated fat, and may have rendered some of us vulnerable to mood problems. A healthy, balanced diet combined with omega-3 and probiotic intake (that is, foods we used to eat more of) could be the foundation on which to build changes to our thinking and behaviour.

Final Thoughts

World-reknowned scientist and long-time sufferer of severe motor-neurone disease, Professor Stephen Hawking, said something very encouraging about clinical depression recently (January 2016). He compared depression with black holes, explaining that no matter how dark they seem, neither are impossible to escape from. Although previously thought of as eternal prisons, he said that things can actually get out of black holes, possibly into another universe. He said that if you feel yourself to be trapped in a black hole, don't give up, you can find your way out.

Helpful words from someone with such knowledge and intellect, who has been physically trapped within his own body for 50 years. I certainly agree that when you emerge out of a depressive episode you enter a new personal universe of sorts. The risk remains that you will get sucked back in again, unwittingly or mistakenly. But if you do, have faith that - providing you persist and chip away at the multifactorial aspects of the illness - you will re-emerge and gain full health again.

Thankyou for reading. Best wishes and stay patient.

#difficultnotimpossible

Main References

- Allen, Jon Dr. *Coping with Depression : From Catch 22 to Hope.* The Menninger Clinic, USA (2006).
- Biddulph, S. *Manhood : An Action Plan to Change Mens' Live (2004).*
- BMA. *New Guide to Medicines and Drugs (2011).*
- BNF. *British National Formulary (2009).*
- Cantopher, Tim. *Depression : The Curse of the Strong (2012).*
- Carlson, Richard. *You Can Feel Good Again* (1993).
- Fujiwara D and Dolan P. *Valuing Mental Health.* UKCP (2014).
- Haig, M. *Reasons to Stay Alive* (2015).
- Healy, D. *Psychiatric Drugs Explained (2004).*
- Lindenfield, G. *Assert Yourself : Simple Steps to Getting What you Want (2001).*
- Milligan, S and Clare, A. *Depression and How to Survive I (1994).*
- Padesky, C and Greenberger, D. *Mind Over Mood* (2000).
- Peck, M Scott. *The Road Less Travelled (1990).*
- Puri BK and Boyd, H. The *Natural Way to Beat Depression* (2004).
- Rowe, Dorothy. *Depression : The Way out of your Prison (2003).*
- Stoll, A. *The Omega-3 Connection (2012).*
- White, J. *Stress Control presentations, NHS Greater Glasgow & Clyde* (2013).
- Williams, C et al. *Overcoming Depression : a Five Areas Approach* (2000).

Figures

Chapter 2, p.38, fig. 1 : *The Johari Window*
Chapter 3, p.65, fig. 2 : Action of Antidepressants on the Neurones of the Brain
Chapter 4, p.79, fig. 3 : *Eatwell Chart*
Chapter 5, p.96, fig. 4 : *Eg of a Thought Record*
Chapter 5, p.100, fig. 5 : *Stress Vulnerability Model*
Chapter 5, p.101, fig. 6 : *Model of Performance vs Anxiety*

Chapter 6, p104, fig. 7 : *CBT Model*
Chapter 6, p.113, fig. 8 : *Continuum of Assertive, Passive and Aggressive*
Chapter 6, p.114, fig. 9 : *Stick Man Diagram of Assertive, Passive & Aggressive*
Chapter 9, p.133, fig. 10 : *"5-a-Day" Wellness Model*

Websites

www.beatingtheblues.co.uk
www.getselfhelp.co.uk
www.livinglifetothefull.com
www.patient.co.uk